~~~ꜫꜳ~~~

In Memoriam:
Glimpses from Indiana's Legal Past

~~~ꜫꜳ~~~

compiled and edited by
Wendy L. Adams
Elizabeth R. Osborn

A publication of the Indiana Supreme Court's
"Courts in the Classroom" project

Indiana Supreme Court
Indianapolis, Indiana

Indiana Supreme Court
Indiana State House
200 West Washington Street,
Indianapolis, IN 46204

A publication of the Indiana Supreme Court's "Courts in the Classroom" project

In association with
IBJ Custom Publishing,
41 E. Washington Street, Suite 200,
Indianapolis, IN 46204
www.ibjcustompublishing.com

Library of Congress Cataloging-in Publication Data

Wendy L. Adams; Elizabeth R. Osborn
       In Memoriam: Glimpses from Indiana's Legal Past

       ISBN 0-9776675-1-0

       ©2006

Cover photos courtesy of The Lincoln Museum, Fort Wayne, Indiana (#46); 1865 Lincoln writing sample from Oliver P. Morton Papers, L113, Manuscript Section, Indiana State Library

Table of Contents

Table of Contents continued...

Introduction

by Chief Justice Shepard

Sprinkled through the several hundred volumes of reported Indiana appellate decisions are scores of entries labeled "In Memoriam." Similar to an obituary, an *In Memoriam* honors a public figure at death. It memorializes the deceased's deeds and accomplishments throughout his or her lifetime.

The idea for this volume grew from such memorials found in a series of books called *Indiana Reports* and *Indiana Cases*, which contain the written opinions of the Indiana Supreme Court. Opinions are usually grouped chronologically and published seriatim. *Indiana Reports* was an official state publication covering opinions written between 1848-1981. The *Indiana Cases*, originally issued by West Publishing Co., overlaps with the *Reports* from 1934-1981 and continues through the present. The first *In Memoriam* in these volumes marked the death of Abraham Lincoln in 1865. The next *In Memoriam* did not appear until almost fifteen years later. Most *In Memoriam* writings appeared between the 1880s and the 1980s.

Nearly all of the men memorialized in this *In Memoriam* (and, yes, they were all men) sat on the Indiana Supreme Court at some point during their lives. These sketches included forty-two Indiana Supreme Court justices, eight Indiana Court of Appeals judges, three prominent Indiana lawyers (two of whom received Presidential appointments), one President of the United States, one Vice-President, and one well-known trial judge.

I hope you enjoy learning more about the accomplishments of these famous Hoosiers, and reading how their colleagues honored them at their passing. This volume is part of a series of publications sponsored by the Indiana Supreme Court through its "Courts in the Classroom" project to educate Hoosiers about Indiana's legal past. You can find information about these publications from the Court's website (www.in.gov/judiciary/citc).

Randall T. Shepard

Randall T. Shepard
Chief Justice of Indiana

Editors' Note

by Wendy L. Adams & Elizabeth R. Osborn

You will note that the editors have organized the men honored in this book in the order in which they were memorialized, instead of listing them alphabetically by last name or chronologically by date of birth. This approach was chosen with the hope that it will help readers place the men, and their contributions, into the larger context of Indiana's and the nation's history. For your convenience, an alphabetical index by last name can be found at the end of the text.

The entry for each honoree contains a portrait, a biographical "fact box," and a copy of the actual *In Memoriam* as it was written and published. Since these are original documents simply reproduced in this publication, original pagination, spelling, and other details were retained. A footnote citation at the bottom of each *In Memoriam* indicates the volume of either the *Indiana Reports* or *Indiana Cases* in which it was originally printed.

Although the memorials in this text are taken exclusively from the *Indiana Reports* and *Indiana Cases*, the *Indiana Appellate Court Reports* also contains several entries honoring prominent figures within the legal community. *Appellate Court Reports* was a publication of the state and included the decisions of Indiana's intermediate appellate court from 1890-1979. In 1971, the reporter was renamed *Indiana Court of Appeals Reports* to reflect a corresponding change in the name of the court. The Court of Appeals *In Memoriam* printed in the *Indiana Cases* after the cessation of the *Indiana Court of Appeals Reports* appear in this volume. Reproducing the *In Memoriam* found in the *Appellate Court Reports* would be a useful future publication.

While much of the biographical information for each entry can be found within the *In Memoriam* itself, the editors relied heavily on *Biographical Sketches of Indiana Supreme Court Justices** to create the fact boxes preceding each document. In addition to this article, the following sources were consulted:

- BIOGRAPHICAL DIRECTORY OF THE UNITED STATES CONGRESS, 1774-2005: www.gpoaccess.gov/serialset/cdocuments/hd108-222/index.html (Gov't Printing Office, 2005).

- A BIOGRAPHICAL DIRECTORY OF THE INDIANA GENERAL ASSEMBLY (Rebecca A. Shepherd et al. eds., The Ind. Historical Bureau) (1980).

- JOHN D. BARNHART & DONALD F. CARMONY, INDIANA: FROM FRONTIER TO INDUSTRIAL COMMONWEALTH (1954).

---

* Minde C. Browning et al., *Biographical Sketches of Indiana Supreme Court Justices*, 30 Ind. L. Rev. 329 (1997). The biographical information contained within the article is also available online through the Indiana Supreme Court's webpage, see http://www.indianacourts.org/Justices/bychron.aspx.

Editors' Note continued...

- *Proceedings of the 35th Annual Meeting of The Indiana State Bar Association, in 7* IND. L.J. 3 (1931-32).

- INDIANAPOLIS MEN OF AFFAIRS (Paul D. Brown ed., The Am. Biographical Soc'y) (1923).

- JACOB P. DUNN, INDIANA AND INDIANANS (1919).

- COURTS AND LAWYERS OF INDIANA (Leander J. Monks ed., 1916).

- B.R. SULGROVE, HISTORY OF INDIANAPOLIS AND MARION COUNTY, Indiana (1884).

Unless otherwise noted, images in this book are from the collection of the Indiana Supreme Court.

The editors would like to thank Gregory S. Knapp, a student at the Indiana University School of Law—Bloomington and Bethany Natali, a public history student at Indiana University Purdue University Indianapolis, for their assistance in preparing the manuscript for publication. In addition, we would like to thank Elizabeth Wilkerson from the Indiana State Library, Manuscripts Division, for her invaluable assistance in this and many other projects.

WLA & ERO

1865 portrait courtesy of Indiana Picture Collection, Manuscript Section, Indiana State Library

Abraham Lincoln

⌒ 1809-1865 ⌒

- Born February 12, 1809, in Hardin County, Kentucky.

- Lived in southern Indiana from 1816 to 1830, then moved to Illinois with his family.

- Served as a captain in the Black Hawk War of 1832.

- Began a career in law in 1836.

- Elected the sixteenth president of the United States in 1860.

- Signed the Emancipation Proclamation on January 1, 1863, granting freedom to slaves in those states which had seceded from the Union.

- Shot by John Wilkes Booth on April 14, 1865, at Ford's Theatre in Washington, D.C.

- Died April 15, 1865, in Washington, D.C.

PROCEEDINGS

OF THE

Supreme Court of the State of Indiana

ON THE ANNOUNCEMENT OF THE

DEATH OF ABRAHAM LINCOLN,

President of the United States.

———•◆•———

At the opening of the court, on the morning of the 20th day of *June*, 1865, the following preamble and resolutions, prepared and adopted at a meeting of the bar of the Supreme Court, were presented by a committee, with the request that they might be spread upon the records of the court :

"The death of ABRAHAM LINCOLN, the President of the *United States*, on the 15th day of last *April*, is an event so startling and sorrowful, that the bar cannot suffer it to pass without offering to the court an expression of their appreciation of his lofty and pure character, in all the relations which he sustained in life ; and of their profound sorrow for his sudden death, under circumstances so horrible as to have shocked the whole civilized world, and overwhelmed the people of his country with a grief at once more universal and heartfelt than they have ever before known.   The bar feel it to be due to themselves and to the court, to give utterance to their sympathy with the universal grief of the nation.   They, therefore, respectfully present the following resolutions to the court, and request that they may be spread upon the records:
1. *Resolved*, That the death of ABRAHAM LINCOLN, President of the *United States*, is a great national calamity, which

nearly and profoundly touches the whole people; that his patient labor and ability, his gentleness and mercy, his unsectional patriotism, and his catholic humanity, are qualities which the country could at any time ill afford to lose; and which, in times like the present, it will be difficult to replace.

2. *Resolved*, That his example, in all the stages of his life, is worthy of imitation by his countrymen, and affords, at the same time, for their encouragement, an assurance that the faithful continuance in well doing will, even in this life, lead to honorable distinction and rewards.

3. *Resolved*, That we tender to the family of the illustrious dead our heartfelt condolence in this night of their affliction and sorrow."

FRAZER, J., in response to the resolutions, said:

I have been requested by my brethren of the bench to say something on this occasion, because I happened to have a slight personal acquaintance with Mr. LINCOLN, before his first nomination for the presidency, and because it is known to them, that my unbounded admiration for his great qualities as a statesman dates prior to the first public suggestion of his name in that connection. For full two years before that event, and before he had entered upon the series of great debates in *Illinois* with the lamented *Douglas*, he seemed to me to be, in all essential respects, the fittest man in the nation for that high office, during that crisis of our national affairs which, it was apparent, could not be much longer delayed, and the most likely to accomplish its correct, and, possibly, peaceful solution. No superior discernment is either shown or claimed in this; it merely happened that I studied him earlier than many others, and the allusion to the fact will be pardoned, I hope, when it is remembered that it cannot but afford me a melancholy pleasure, as I seek to contribute one sprig of myrtle to that unfading chaplet with which the nation and the world will crown his memory.

Proceedings on the announcement of the death of President Lincoln.

Mr. LINCOLN possessed certain traits of character in a remarkable degree, which could not fail to be perceived, and which won for him the personal esteem of almost every one. His great kindness of heart, his transparent and child-like honesty, the simplicity of his tastes and habits, his deep sympathy with the common people, his unfaltering faith that the GOD of the nations would not allow the Union of these States to be now destroyed, and that he was himself an instrument in Divine hands for the accomplishment of this purpose, his unselfishness, and his unfailing fund of good humor—these are as well understood now as they can ever be in the future, and they contributed largely to his great popularity, and enabled him to discharge unpleasant duties without giving pain or offense, and to unite the country in executing measures now seen to have been wise and necessary, but which, at the time, did not fully meet the general approbation.

But for the confidence which these qualities inspired in his motives and the rectitude of his purposes, the people of the north, jealous of the incroachments of power, might not have submitted to the exercise of that large amount of authority on his part, without which it is probable that we would have failed to suppress the rebellion and have ceased to be numbered amongst the nations.

But he had other qualities contributing, even in a much larger measure, to constitute him, as he was, in my judgment, the first statesman of this age, and the peer of any whom the world has yet produced.

He was always self-possessed. He never lost control of his great faculties, by the influence of excitement or passion. What ruler wielded power in such stormy times? Who ever held the helm of government, when such tremendous forces were hurled against the state; when such a tempest of passion prevailed around him; when such fearful breakers rose up on every side, and when he scarcely knew that the fidelity of any of his crew could be depended upon, and when mutiny was almost every where? And

524 SUPREME COURT OF INDIANA.

yet calmly, though firmly, he held the ship on her course, watchful of every peril, ready for any danger, with a suitable plan for every emergency, and a dauntless, cheerful, hopeful, persistent confidence, which gave courage to every true man about it. And, during all this, no word of hate or malice towards any escaped his lips, and not a single act of harshness, or of mere vengeance, was he provoked to do during the whole of his administration! Amongst the rulers of the world, there is found no parallel to this, except the single case of WASHINGTON, and even he was sometimes betrayed into a terrible outburst of anger.

Mr. LINCOLN was self-reliant and firm, without stubbornness. We have had no president since *Jackson* who was not controlled by his cabinet, and possibly none who had not selected greater men than himself for his counsellors. Mr. LINCOLN called about him the greatest men of his party—*Seward, Chase, Cameron* and *Bates*, all the competitors he had had in the convention which had nominated him. He availed himself of their advice and counsel; they often differed, it is said, upon the most important measures. He deliberately weighed every suggestion, and decided finally for himself, often even against the wishes of his own party; and having once decided, he adhered to his convictions against whatever influences were invoked to change them.

But I think that the quality for which, more than any other, history will distinguish him, was the greatness of his intellect. Distant nations, less familiar than we are with his goodness which won our love, and his integrity which commanded our confidence, and which have not been stirred by the passions which this fearful civil war engendered here, are now better situated to appreciate this quality than we are—and this is their verdict: That he has shown himself to be amongst the wisest rulers of modern times. He was without early advantages, and labored under the difficulties of a defective education. His boyhood and early manhood were not devoted to the training of his faculties, and the development of their powers.

MAY TERM, 1865. 525

Proceedings on the announcement of the death of President Lincoln.

And yet I know of no speaker or writer, of the present or the past, who could so thoroughly strip a subject of everything which did not belong to it, and then discuss the subject itself with so much clearness, and exhaust it with so much brevity. And this, to my mind, is the highest proof of intellectual greatness. A clear discrimination, and an accurate perception of things, which constitute the very bone and sinew of intellect, were thus pre-eminently manifested in his character.

Of the wisdom of his measures, so far as any of them have accomplished their full results, there is probably, even now, no two opinions. Of others, which have not yet yielded their fruits, it is impossible now to speak with absolute certainty; but I think that so far, they are each passing day commanding more and more the approval of all intelligent and good men, who at first either doubted or opposed them.

That such a man should have been slain by an assassin, in the interests of the rebellion, after it was clearly seen that the national authority would be speedily restored, awakened a deeper and more universal sorrow, and a sincere and more general public manifestation of grief than has often occurred amongst men. I know not why the God who seemed to guide him in the discharge of his difficult duties, and who could have stricken down the assassin before he did the damnable deed, yet permitted it to be done. But I do know one of the lessons to be learned from it, by all who will receive plain instruction. It may be useful in the future. It would have saved us the lost ones of the last four years, if we had learned it long ago. It is this: that the spirit of the rebellion was execrable beyond measure; that the terrors of the past four years closely bordered on the infernal, and that in dealing with its instigators, originators and leaders as criminals, mere sympathy for *them*, if it shall interfere with the purpose to make the state secure against them and their teachings in the future, will not be mercy, but will be almost itself a crime.

526   SUPREME COURT OF INDIANA.

ELLIOTT, C. J.—*Gentlemen of the Bar:* In responding to your resolutions, I shall not attempt to pronounce a eulogy upon either the life, character or public services of our lamented President. If time and opportunity were afforded, and I were competent to the task, still it would seem superfluous, as I could scarcely expect, after all that has been said and published, to express a new thought, or add a single leaf to the chaplet that crowns his memory. Indeed, he is so enshrined in the hearts of the people, that every patriot's bosom swells with honest praise, more eloquent than language can express.

Under any circumstances, the death of the Chief Magistrate of the nation would be regarded by all as a public bereavement, and would produce general sadness and sorrow. But the death of ABRAHAM LINCOLN by the hand of an assassin, and in view of the motive for the act, and the circumstances which surrounded both the victim and the deed, filled every mind with amazement and consternation, and every heart with inexpressible sorrow and grief. A nation most deeply mourns the loss of its Chief Executive, whom the people had learned to appreciate, honor and love, and their grief is swelled to indignation and horror at the foul manner of his death.

Mr. LINCOLN was the immediate victim of the assassin's blow, but the wound is national, for it is felt by all.

The people are shocked and angered, because they loathe and detest the most wicked crime that terminated the President's life. They are stricken with the deepest sorrow, because a great and good ruler, whom they loved, and in whom they confided, has fallen in his successful labors for the preservation of his country.

To the nation, the life of ABRAHAM LINCOLN was most precious. As an instrument of Divine Providence, he had substantially accomplished a great mission, that will render his name immortal, and cause his memory to be hallowed by all future generations. To finite minds it would seem peculiarly fitting, if not essential, that he should have lived

MAY TERM, 1865.   527

to have finished his good work, so nearly accomplished, and to enjoy the full realization of its blessings. But it is otherwise, and we bow in humble submission to Him who controls the destinies of all things. Yet, as " out of the fullness of the heart the mouth speaketh," it is meet that we give full utterance to our feelings of sorrow.

When we remember the broad humanity and great kindness of heart of Mr. LINCOLN, so universally acknowledged and appreciated, it is impossible to conceive that the assassin was impelled to the act by any feeling of personal hatred or revenge toward him; or to believe that its immediate perpetrator is alone responsible for the wicked and fatal deed. The blow was undoubtedly aimed at the life of the government, of which the President was the chosen representative, and, therefore, the selected victim. And whilst we mourn his loss as a great national bereavement, we yet have cause to rejoice in the fact that the government still lives. That it has survived the terrible assaults of a wicked and powerful rebellion, and successfully maintained a desperate struggle for existence, lasting for a period of more than four years, and still retains vitality sufficient to withstand this last unnatural and unexpected shock, affords gratifying evidence, to every loyal and reflecting mind, of the wisdom and justice of its nicely balanced machinery, and of its ability for self protection and preservation.

A lesson is also taught in the fact that, to the author of the crime, just retribution swiftly followed his foul deed. Though he escaped immediate arrest, yet, ere the mortal remains of his honored victim were deposited in their place of final rest, he had ceased to be, and his own remains were hid forever from mortal sight. And, for myself, I may be permitted to say that I trust the world may never know what particular spot of earth is stained by the secret.

ORDERED, that the resolutions be spread upon the records of the court, and that, out of respect to the memory of the deceased Chief Magistrate of the nation, this court do now adjourn.

Samuel Hamilton Buskirk

1820-1879

- Born January 19, 1820, in New Albany, Floyd County, Indiana.

- Moved to Bloomington, Monroe County, Indiana, in 1831, where he attended school and college.

- Graduated from Indiana University School of Law in 1841.

- Served as Monroe County recorder from 1844 to 1845.

- Began the practice of law in 1848.

- Elected to the Indiana House of Representatives for five different terms between 1848 and 1865, serving as Speaker of the House in 1863 and 1864.

- Served as Monroe County prosecuting attorney in 1851.

- Elected to the Indiana Supreme Court in 1874, serving from January 3, 1875, to January 1, 1877.

- Served as president of the Indiana State Bar Association in 1876.

- Died April 3, 1879, in Indianapolis, Marion County, Indiana.

IN MEMORIAM.

"The members of the Bar of Indiana and the Bar Association of Indianapolis, now assembled, express their profound sorrow for the loss of their friend and brother, the Honorable SAMUEL H. BUSKIRK.

"Judge BUSKIRK departed this life at his residence in the city of Indianapolis, on the evening of the third day of April. 1879, in the sixtieth year of his age. He was a native of Indiana, and his entire life was spent within its limits. He was a man of marked ability, and attained the highest positions in the legislative and judicial service of the State. His public life terminated with his retirement from the bench of the Supreme Court. His decisions place him among the distinguished jurists of the country. As a statesman, lawyer and citizen, Judge BUSKIRK, in a large measure, enjoyed and deserved the confidence and respect of his fellow citizens.

"He was laborious in his profession, painstaking in the performance of his duties, and was a courteous, genial gentleman in all the relations of life.

"His example is worthy of imitation by his surviving brethren; and they tender to his bereaved family their profound sympathy.

"The Committee report the following resolution:

"*Resolved,* That the several courts of the county of Marion, and the Supreme Court of Indiana, be requested to enter the foregoing memorial upon their records, and that the secretary of this meeting furnish a copy of the same to the family of our deceased brother."

Upon the presentation to the Supreme Court of the proceedings of the members of the Bar of Indiana, and of the Bar Association of Indianapolis, at a meeting held on the fifth day of April, 1879, to express their sentiments of sorrow for the loss of their friend and brother, the

(601)

602 IN MEMORIAM.

Hon. Samuel Hamilton Buskirk, Hon. George V. Howk, then Chief Justice, on behalf of the Court, said:

The Judges of this Court desire to unite with the Bar of Indiana, and the Bar Association of Indianapolis, in their tribute of respect to the memory of their departed friend and brother, the Honorable Samuel H. Buskirk. We have known him long and well; while he was a judge of this court, some of us were his brother judges, while others of our number were his associates in other walks of public life. We all bear willing testimony to the many good and noble qualities of his head and heart. Gifted by nature with an intellect above the average, by close application and unwearied labor, he won the highest office in the profession of his choice, in his native State; and, having won, he adorned the position by his devotion to the discharge of duty, and his learning as a jurist. His treatise on the Practice on Appeals in this Court has been, and will continue to be, of great benefit to his brothers, at the bar and on the bench; and by them his name will not be forgotten.

The proceedings and resolutions of the Bar of this State, and of the Bar Association of Indianapolis, express sentiments and opinions in regard to our deceased friend and brother, in which we fully concur; and they will be entered at length upon the order-book of this Court.

Samuel Elliott Perkins
1811-1879

- Born December 6, 1811, in Brattleboro, Vermont.
- Orphaned at the age of five and raised by friends in Massachusetts.
- Read law in New York.
- Moved to Richmond, Wayne County, Indiana, in 1836.
- Admitted to the bar and opened a law office in Richmond in 1837.
- Became editor of the *Richmond Jeffersonian*, a Democratic paper, in 1837, and again from 1839 to 1840.
- Appointed prosecutor by Indiana Governor Whitcomb in 1843.
- Served on the Indiana Supreme Court under both the first and second Indiana constitutions, from January 1, 1846, to January 3, 1865.
- Taught law at Northwestern Christian University (now known as Butler University) at Indianapolis, Marion County, Indiana, in 1857 and then Indiana University from 1870 to 1872.
- Served on the Indiana Supreme Court a second time from January 1, 1877, to December 17, 1879.
- Died December 17, 1879, in Indianapolis, Marion County, Indiana.

In Memoriam.

On the 26th day of May, 1880, the following memorial in regard to the death of the Hon. SAMUEL E. PERKINS, who died December 17th, 1879, at Indianapolis, was presented to the Supreme Court of Indiana. Its presentation was prefaced with the following remarks by Napoleon B. Taylor, Esq.:

" *May it Please Your Honors:*

" To be able to speak with candor, in terms of praise, of a professional brother, gives pleasure.

" The worthy member of the legal profession, without exception, while in life commands the highest respect and fullest confidence, and generally shares in the rewards that are due to and bestowed upon the meritorious, in every calling.

" When such a one has passed from his labors to that rest which awaits us all, it has been a custom, long established and sacredly observed, to make a public declaration of the esteem in which he was held by his professional brethren, and to place upon the records of the courts a memorial of his merit and services that may be as lasting as those records themselves.

" This custom is not peculiar to our profession of the law, but is largely practised by those who follow other pursuits and form divisions of the grand army of laborers in the interest and advancement of humanity and of human affairs.

" With us it is esteemed a duty not only, but a debt also, due the memory of the departed, and a solace to his surviving family and friends, as well as a sharp incentive to noble emulation and lofty endeavor on the part of those of his professional brethren who survive, and to such as afterward engage in the study and practice of the law, to cheer them in the arduous work, with the hope that they, too, may win like honor and renown, and, at the end, the same recorded and durable mention.

(601)

602 ## IN MEMORIAM.

" It has been the fortune of but one member of our profession in this State to attain and hold, for such a length of time, so high a rank in her judiciary as Hon. SAMUEL E. PERKINS. That one was Hon. Isaac Blackford, who, for more than thirty-five years continuously, filled a seat upon the bench of this Court; and, after his retirement from it, was, in the year 1855, commissioned one of the judges of the United States Court of Claims, at the city of Washington, and died there on the 31st day of December, 1859, while holding that office.

" On the 21st day of January, in the year 1846, SAMUEL E. PERKINS was appointed by Hon. James Whitcomb, who was then Governor of this State, a judge of this Court, to succeed Hon. Jeremiah Sullivan, whose term of office had expired.

" Governor Whitcomb was a lawyer of high standing in his profession, and Judge Sullivan was regarded as a man of spotless integrity, and esteemed one of the ablest jurists in the Commonwealth. The appointment, therefore, of Judge PERKINS to succeed Judge Sullivan was looked upon as a very high compliment.

" This appointment reached to the end of the next General Assembly, and on the 29th day of January, in the year 1847, Judge PERKINS was appointed and commissioned a judge of this Court for the term of seven years, from the end of the General Assembly then in session.

" The constitution of 1816 was in force at that time, and, by its provisions, the judges of this Court were appointed by the Governor, by and with the advice and consent of the Senate, and the full term of their appointment was one year longer than it is under our present Constitution.

" Before the expiration of this term of seven years, for which he had been appointed, the constitution of 1852 (our present constitution) was adopted and went into force. This constitution changed the mode of selecting judges. It introduced the system of choosing them by popular vote, and under its provisions an election for judges of this Court was held on the 12th day of October of that year, and Judge PERKINS, who had received the nomination of the Democratic party over Hon. Isaac Blackford, was elected for the full term of six years.

" At the State election, on the 12th day of October, in the year 1858, Judge PERKINS, who had again received the nomination of his party for this high office, was reelected for the further term of six years.

JUDGE SAMUEL E. PERKINS.   603

" This term expired on the 3d day of January, 1865, and Judge PERKINS, who was defeated with his party at the general election in October, 1864, retired from the bench and resumed the practice of the law in the city of Indianapolis, and continued in the practice until the 24th day of Augnst, in the year 1872, when he was appointed by His Excellency Conrad Baker, the then Governor of this State, to succeed Hon. Frederick Rand, who had resigned, on the bench of the Superior Court of Marion County.

" Judge PERKINS accepted this appointment, and, at the State election in the ensuing October, he was elected, without opposition, for a full term of four years. This highly honorable, and during that time very laborious, position was filled by Judge PERKINS until the close of the year 1876, and on the 3d day of January, 1877, he passed to the bench of this court, to which he had been elected at the State election in the month of October, 1876, where he continued to serve until the date of his death, the 17th day of December, 1879.

" His service as a judge of this Court was continuous from the 21st day of January, 1846, to the 3d day of January, 1865, lacking a few days only of nineteen years, and which, added to his last service, wanted but a small fraction of twenty-two years; and if he had lived until the end of the term for which he was last elected, and a part of which he had served, would have covered near the full fourth of a century.

" Although the period of Judge PERKINS' service, as a judge of this court, was exceeded in length by that of Judge Blackford, yet, in the marked changes and in the strange and stirring events which took place and followed each other in quick succession, and in the new, important and difficult questions that came up to be examined and passed upon, it far surpassed, in interest and importance, that comprised in the term of Judge Blackford.

" Of the industry which distinguished Judge PERKINS' career on the bench, and the ability displayed by him in the discharge of his high trust, during all this time, it is not necessary to speak. The opinions prepared and delivered by him, contained in thirty-nine volumes of our State reports, which are familiar to Your Honors and to the members of the legal profession in this State, are sufficient evidence of that labor, research and talent.

" But the memorial which I hold in my hand, to be presented to this Court, speaks of these matters, and of all

604 IN MEMORIAM.

others affecting his relations in life necessary to be mentioned or referred to in this presentation, in words forcible, distinct and impartial, and which become the occasion.

"He was blessed with length of days. The days of the years of his life reached almost the allotted time of three score years and ten; and his labors continued until near the end.

"It can hardly be deemed exaggeration for me to say that he fell like a soldier—died at his post—crowned with the honors of his profession, and holding at the time its highest trust in the State.

"At a meeting of the Bar Association of the city of Indianapolis, called after his death, which was held in the court-house on the 19th day of December, in the year 1879, and participated in by the members of the bar of this State then in that city, this memorial was adoped. By a resolution passed at that meeting, it was made my duty to present this memorial to this Court, and to ask that it be spread upon its records, which I now do, with the wish that those records and this memorial may be as lasting as the ages."

The memorial referred to in the foregoing remarks, and presented to the court, is in these words:

"Again, in the history of the State, death has entered the Supreme Court and made vacant a seat upon its bench. The late Chief Justice is dead. We meet to do suitable honor to the name and memory, and mourn the death, of Judge SAMUEL E. PERKINS. His eminent success is an encouragement, his death an admonition. Endowed with strong and active faculties, he pursued the purposes of his life with fortitude and determination, and at the close of his career he stood among the distinguished of a profession in which distinction must be merited to be achieved. He was successful in life, and attained exalted position and enjoyed the admiration and approval of his countrymen, not only because of his excellent natural endowments, but also because his faculties were cultivated and developed by diligent labor, and beautified by extensive and useful learning, and also because his motives were pure and his conduct upright. In this we have a lesson and an encouragement. The people gave him high honor and made it as enduring as the laws and records of the State. His name is forever interwoven in our judicial history. So long as society shall remain organized under the government of law will the student of laws consult his opinions and decisions. Through

JUDGE SAMUEL E. PERKINS.   605

coming generations will his labor and learning influence
both the legislator and judge. He was an able and a
faithful judge, and brought honor on our profession. We
will cherish his memory. In his death we are admonished
that no earthly distinction can defeat or postpone the
'inevitable hour.' 'The paths of glory lead but to the
grave.' To his family and kindred we extend our sympathy."

BIDDLE, C. J., on behalf of the Court, made the following response:

"The members of this Bench are in full sympathy with
the members of the Bar, and the more immediate friends,
in mourning for the dead.

"He has gone, but his works remain. No one has done
more, or done it better, than the deceased. He came to the
Bench early, and remained late. Death found him enjoying its highest honor. Judge PERKINS occupied this
Bench during that interesting transition period while the
the mode of administering justice was passing from the
common law practice to the present code of procedure, and
by his ability, industry and energy, was a most useful member of the Court. He also occupied this Bench during the
most critical period in the history of the United States—the
late Civil War—when American institutions were strained
to their utmost tension, yet found themselves sufficient to
protect State Governments—the Many; and to maintain
the Government of the Union—the One. Whatever differences of opinion among patriots there might have been
then, that the course of Judge PERKINS was fearless, independent and upright, is not now doubted by any.

"His name deserves to live while constitutional liberty is
secure, while equal laws are respected, while the administration of justice is honored, and as long as the homage
of the living is due to the worth of the dead.

"Your memorial shall be written amongst the records of
this Court at the close of the labors of the deceased, to
bear perpetual testimony of the esteem and honor in which
he is held by the members of the bench and the bar who
survive him, and who knew him so long and so well."

Image courtesy of Manuscript Section, Indiana State Library.

Horatio Cooley Newcomb

1821-1882

- Born December 20, 1821, in Wellsboro, Pennsylvania.

- Moved with his parents to Indiana in June 1833.

- Studied as a saddler's apprentice from 1836 to 1838.

- Read law with his uncle at Vernon, Jennings County, Indiana, in 1841.

- Admitted to the bar in 1844.

- Practiced law in Jennings County, Indiana, from 1844 to 1846.

- Moved to Indianapolis, Marion County, Indiana, and formed a partnership with Ovid Butler, founder of Northwestern Christian University (now known as Butler University), in 1846.

- Elected mayor of Indianapolis, serving from 1849 to 1851.

- Elected to the Indiana House of Representatives in 1851.

Continued

Horatio Cooley Newcomb

continued

- Elected to the Indiana Senate in 1861, resigning after the special session.

- Joined the 107th Regiment, Indiana Volunteers, which was organized on July 12, 1863, to repel the Morgan Raid during the Civil War, and mustered out seven days later holding the rank of sergeant.

- Elected to a second and third term to the Indiana House of Representatives in 1865 and 1867.

- Edited the *Indianapolis State Journal* from 1864 to 1868.

- Appointed Marion Superior Court judge in 1871, then elected to the same position in 1874.

- Worked as Indiana Supreme Court commissioner from 1881 until his death.

- Died May 23, 1882, in Indianapolis, Marion County, Indiana.

In Memoriam.

On the 26th day of May, 1882, the following memorials in regard to the death of the HON. HORATIO C. NEWCOMB, who died at Indianapolis, Indiana, on May 23d, 1882, were presented to the Supreme Court of Indiana:

"The surviving members of the Supreme Court Commission beg leave to present to the court, the following memorial of their late distinguished associate, the HON. HORATIO C. NEWCOMB:

"His public life and services are too well known and appreciated to need any mention here. Appointed a member of our commission in April, 1881, he had been with us less than a year, when compelled by declining health to abandon our meetings, but in that brief time he had won our affection by his genial and kindly nature, and had secured our entire admiration and respect by his ability as a lawyer and a judge. He was a remarkably sound, clear-headed, sagacious man; we shall miss his valuable aid in the discharge of our duties; we shall miss his attractive companionship. We mourn his loss, but we remember that he died in the midst of his usefulness, an honor to his profession and to this court. We ask that this tribute to his memory be placed upon the record of the court.　　　　　"GEORGE A. BICKNELL, C. C.

"JOHN MORRIS,

"WILLIAM M. FRANKLIN,

"JAMES I. BEST."

Memorial of the Indianapolis Bar Association, presented by HONS. J. W. GORDON, L. HOWLAND, O. B. HORD and A. C. HARRIS, committee, and address of Judge B. K. ELLIOTT:

"HORATIO COOLEY NEWCOMB was born at Wellsboro, Pa., on December 20th, 1821, and died at Indianapolis, Ind., on May 23d, 1882. He commenced the study of the law in 1841, and was admitted to the bar of the Supreme Court of this State

(601)

602   IN MEMORIAM.

in 1844.   He commenced the practice of his profession in the
town of Vernon, but in 1846 he removed to Indianapolis, and
entered into partnership with Ovid Butler, one of the most
successful lawyers of that day in central Indiana.   Since 1846,
with the exception of a few years in which his talent for general politics and his vigorous pen led him into the editorial
chair of the Indianapolis Journal, his life has been spent at the
bar, on the bench, or in some responsible official position.
For five years he was one of the judges of the Superior Court
of Marion county, and, after retiring from that bench, he resumed, so far as his health permitted, the practice of the law,
and continued it until, in 1881, he was appointed one of the
Commissioners of the Supreme Court, which position he held
at his death.

" Judge NEWCOMB was a man of clear mind, great industry
and perfect integrity.   His grasp of a question, while perhaps
slower than that of some of more than ordinary brilliancy of
perception, was firm, comprehensive and just.   The whole
position, with all its lights and shades, would open before him
as a result not alone of his mental power, but of his unflagging
industry as well.   The subject of his thought was taken up,
not to be laid down until mastered and a conclusion reached.
His honesty of mind and his moral principles were such that
he never shrank from a conclusion because it was distasteful
or unexpected.   A conviction became with him a motive.

"As a lawyer, he was candid with his client, laborious and
untiring in his client's cause, honest with the court, and successful beyond the average of the bar.

"As a judge, he carried to the bench all the industry which
distinguished him in his legal practice, and a ripened intellect,
a clear judgment of the human motives, an impartiality which
could never be doubted, and a knowledge of affairs without
which a judge must always fail in the estimation of the profession.   His conduct toward the bar was of a nature which
the natural justice of his character could not fail to produce.
Courteous to every one, careful not to give unnecessary of-
fence, he sought to preserve the rights of all suitors as things
not to be disposed of in whim or irritation.

"In legislative affairs he was noted for the same personal
characteristics.   While the opponents of the party to which
he was attached might dispute the policy he favored, his vigor,
his tact, his honesty of purpose, his true patriotism never
were questioned.

"As a citizen, his life was quiet and adorned with the virtues of the Christian character.   Domestic in his tastes and

IN MEMORIAM. 603

habits, he was the center of an affectionate family group, and abounded in personal friendships.

"By his death the State has lost a faithful public servant, the bench a just.judge, the bar an honest man, and his family a devoted husband and father.

"JOSHUA G. ADAMS,   F. RAND,
"W. A. KETCHAM,   W. Q. GRESHAM,
"C. C. HINES,   JOHN MORRIS."

Remarks of Judge ELLIOTT on presenting the memorial to the Bar Association of Indianapolis:

"MR. CHAIRMAN—For more than thirty years HORATIO C. NEWCOMB occupied a high place in the affections and confidence of our people. Confidence was never more worthily bestowed. Entrusted with many public offices, he was faithful in all. A purer public and private life than his no man ever lived. It is spotless in its spiritual purity. His earnest, strong nature made him sometimes a fierce political combatant, and involved him in hot and angry controversies, but yet against his integrity and honor no word was ever uttered. The bitterness of partisan strife did not attack his integrity; that passed unchallenged, because impregnable. His opponents never questioned his motives, however much they condemned his j dgment. Judge NEWCOMB was a man of strong convictions. He was for the right, as the right seemed to him, with all the intense earnestness of a great soul. When he had deliberately reached a judgment, whether in matters of religion, politics or law, he adhered to it with unyielding firmness. And yet, so admirable were his qualities of mind and heart, he was neither a fanatic nor a bigot. Firm in adhering to his own conception of right, his enlightened and charitable mind made him careful of the rights of others. His own judgment he obeyed, that of others he respected. He was modest, yet not timid. He was courageous in the avowal of his opinions, and bold in maintaining them. He was an aggressive debater on the hustings, in the legislative halls, and in the forum. Of his own merits and powers he was not sufficiently appreciative; he rated them far below their value. Had he been more of an egotist, he would, I believe, have attained a much higher position than he did; but, after all, there was a noble simplicity in his character that was greater honor than any office could have conferred.

"In his friendships, Judge NEWCOMB was warm and sincere. He made new friends less readily than many, but he never lost any old ones. Many have been more demonstra-

604   IN MEMORIAM.

tive in their friendship than he, few more constant and sincere. He was slow to make friends, but strong to keep them.
His manner was, I am told, somewhat cold and distant. I
can not recollect that it ever seemed so to me. If it ever
did, long years of close friendship and intercourse have driven
the impression from my mind. For these many years he has
seemed to me, what in truth he was, a man of keen sensibili-
ties, of warm emotions and affectionate nature. He was tender and kind, although sometimes stern and almost harsh.
He heartily hated a wicked act, and as heartily believed in
vigorously punishing the evil-doer. Dishonesty and shuffling
in business, in politics or in judicial proceedings aroused his
indignation and produced a storm of invective that was almost terrible. Yet he was not a hard man; there was really
not a bit of flint in his nature. His sympathies were easily
aroused. He was as tender-hearted as a woman, and the suf-
fering and distressed found in him a benefactor and a friend.

  "Judge NEWCOMB'S mind was powerful and massive. It
was solid, not brilliant; but still there were rich veins of humor which oftentimes made his mental productions snap and
sparkle. His perceptive faculties were unusually strong and
vigorous. His mental vision was penetrating and far-seeing.
He saw through the crust to the substance, and he saw not
one side, but all sides. His intellectual grasp was broad and
strong; it took up many things, took strong hold of them,
and retained them until they were examined from many sides.
This great analytical power enabled him to arrange and ad-
just the different parts of an involved and difficult question
so that it could be readily understood and fully mastered.
He was too intensely in earnest to care much for the graces
of oratory. It must, indeed, be owned that a lack or, perhaps, defect of imagination prevented him from ever becoming, in the highest sense, an orator or an advocate. If he
never attained great eloquence, he always spoke well, and
with the strength of a logician. If he was not brilliant, he
was solid. If he did not charm by the graces of his style, he
always talked common sense. He never mistook the false for
the true eloquence. Like all earnest men he hated shams. A
sham was a sham to him whether in advocacy or elsewhere.

  "HORATIO C. NEWCOMB possessed in an eminent degree
the qualities of a great judge. Above all things else was his
sterling honesty. He loved fair play. No suitor ever received
less than that at his hands. He was singularly free from
passion or prejudice. His judicial judgments were the products of an unbiased mind; nothing warped it. He gave to

IN MEMORIAM. 605

every case a full and impartial consideration; no influence turned him from the path of duty. It often seemed to me that such was the character of his mind, and such his habits of thought, that he could not have turned aside if he would. His was a trained legal mind. His logic was severe. His premises were assumed only after careful investigation, and, once established, his conclusions were inevitable. It was a well stored mind. Its stores were not of cases, but of principles. His opinions are models of pure, clean and vigorous judicial style. They are not wanting in elegance, and they are rich in pure idiomatic English.

"The hand that penned these opinions will write no more. The great Judge, in whose decrees there is never error, pronounced the judgment which has taken from us our brother and our friend. We feel sure that at the bar of that last Grand Assize our brother will appear without fear, for through all the years of his life

"He has kept
The whiteness of his soul."

Upon the presentation of the memorials, it was ordered by the Court, that they be spread upon the record; and, as they are so full and just that nothing remains to be added, they are accepted as the expression of the court's appreciation of the noble life and character of Judge NEWCOMB, and of the sincere sorrow of its members for the great loss sustained by his death.

James Lorenzo Worden

1819-1884

- Born May 10, 1819, in Sandisfield, Massachusetts.

- Moved with his widowed mother to Portage County, Ohio, in 1827.

- Studied law with Thomas L. Strait of Cincinnati, Ohio, in 1838.

- Admitted to the Ohio bar in 1841.

- Moved to Columbia City, Whitley County, Indiana, in 1844.

- Appointed prosecuting attorney for the Tenth Judicial Circuit from 1851 to 1852.

- Appointed circuit court judge in 1855, resigning in 1858.

- Served on the Indiana Supreme Court for two non-consecutive terms, 1858 to 1865 and 1871 to 1882.

- Died June 10, 1884, in Fort Wayne, Allen County, Indiana.

In Memoriam.

At the opening of the November Term, 1884, of the Supreme Court, Judge JOHN MORRIS, of Fort Wayne, on behalf of the bar of the State, submitted the following address:

" IF THE COURT PLEASE: It is not the purpose of the bar in this address, even imperfectly, to sketch the life and public services of Hon. JAMES L. WORDEN, who departed this life at 9 : 30 o'clock P. M., on the evening of the 2d of June, 1884. When some one shall have written the history of the people of Indiana, and adequately traced the growth and progress of their civil customs and institutions, then, not sooner perhaps, will the great value of his public services become generally and fully known and appreciated.   And then, if not before, among the opinions of judges who have passed away, and of those who are still living, the judicial opinions of him whose life we would fittingly commemorate, will recall to the minds of judges, of lawyers, and of all who may come after us, the name of one of the purest, the ablest and the wisest of judges, whose judicial labors contributed largely to the social order, security and well-being of the people of the State.

" It is the purpose of the bar rather to give some expression to the sense of the great loss which each member feels and has sustained in his death, to present, though inadequately it may be, their appreciation of the deceased as a man, as a friend and brother, who has long been engaged with them in the administration of public justice.

" Judge WORDEN was born May 10th, 1819, at Sandisfield, Berkshire county, Massachusetts, and was at the time of his death a few days over sixty-five years of age.   His father

(603)

604 ## IN MEMORIAM.

died when he was but eight years old. Soon thereafter he moved with his mother to Portage county, Ohio, where he worked on the farm for the support of the family for several years. He had no educational advantages other than such as the common schools of the neighborhood afforded. He read but few books, but such as he could get were thoroughly read and understood. As a boy, he was curious and inquiring and soon gave evidence to those around him of that clear and penetrating insight into things which he so conspicuously displayed in after life. At the age of nineteen, through the advice of a few appreciating friends, he commenced the study of law in the office of Thomas J. Straight at Cincinnati. In 1841 he was admitted to the bar of the Supreme Court of Ohio. In 1844, after practicing law a few years in Ohio, he moved to Whitley county, Indiana.

" In the spring of 1845 he married Anna Grable. With this excellent and estimable lady, who almost worshipped him, and whom he so tenderly loved, he lived in perfect conjugal happiness until his death.

" The year after his marriage he moved with his young wife to Noble county, where he practiced law until 1849, when he came to Fort Wayne. Here, in company with the late Judge McMahon, and afterwards with the late Hon. Charles Case, he had a large and lucrative practice. Though clear and always forcible, he was not an eloquent speaker; but as a trial lawyer he seemed to be unrivalled in resources, so that he soon came to be regarded as one of the ablest lawyers at the bar. No one at the bar of northern Indiana stood higher than he.

" The deceased was in 1848 selected prosecuting attorney of the tenth judicial circuit. He discharged the duties of this office with eminent ability and success. In 1856, through the unanimous solicitation of the bar, the deceased was appointed by Governor Wright judge of the tenth judicial circuit. By this appointment Judge WORDEN was brought into his proper sphere. Then all who knew him as a *nisi prius* judge, as all who knew him as such at the time of his death, felt and knew how pre-eminently he was fitted for the discharge of judicial functions.

IN MEMORIAM.   605

" His mind was clear, vigorous, penetrating, and singularly
logical and judicial.   No sophistry could mislead him ; mere
plausibility, however specious, never deceived him. He could
separate, with the utmost facility and certainty, the incidental
from the essential facts, so that he who was in the right rarely,
if ever, had occasion to complain of the finding of a jury that
he had charged upon the law and the facts. To him, his conclusions were so clear that they amounted to convictions ;
hence, while he always had great respect for the opinions of
the jury, yet, when convinced that the finding was wrong, he
would promptly set the verdict aside, without the least hesi-
tation.   No man was less wilful than Judge WORDEN, yet few
had more will power than he. He adhered to his conclusions
with great firmness, not because they were his, but because
of the clearness with which he had reached them.   No judge
ever listened more patiently than he did, especially to the
party who seemed to him to be in error. And for this reason
a re-argument of a question once decided was rarely asked.
As a general rule, the party against whom he decided was
satisfied, quite as ready to yield the contest as was his more
fortunate opponent.   It was these qualities, as well as his extensive learning, his patience, his courteous bearing towards
every one of us, and his vivacious and genial spirit and good-
will toward all, that made us all believe that he was the best
nisi prius judge in the State.

" In 1858 Judge WORDEN was appointed by Governor Wil-
lard to fill the vacancy on the Supreme bench occasioned by
the resignation of Judge Stuart.   In 1859 he was elected
to the same position.   He was again elected to the Supreme
bench in 1870, and re-elected in 1876. In 1882, though urged
by his associate judges, and the leading members of the bar
of the State to become a candidate for re-election, he declined,
and was elected by the unanimous vote of the people judge
of the superior court of Allen county.   The deceased served
as judge of the Supreme Court some nineteen years. Through
his labors as one of the judges of the highest court of the
State he will be known and appreciated by those who are to
follow him and us.

606   IN MEMORIAM.

" As has been fittingly remarked by his distinguished successor on the Supreme Bench, his reported opinions will constitute an enduring monument to his memory, handing down his fame and his worth to remote generations.

" No man was ever better fitted for the bench, by his mental constitution than the deceased. He was habitually reflective and thoughtful; his mind, though active, was serene and calm—free from disturbing excitement, and therefore, without bias or prejudice. His power of logical analysis was very acute, so much so that he always saw clearly and without difficulty the precise question to be considered, and was able to separate from it everything that was foreign to it. He saw with great clearness the true relation and just dependence of ideas and things. It was for these reasons that his decisions seemed to carry in themselves the weight of authority. He had great respect for the decisions and opinions of eminent judges, yet he did not always recognize precedents as authority. It was only when supported by reason and founded upon principle that he assented to the authority of adjudged cases. His mind was broad, comprehensive, direct and fair. He saw the point to be decided, and his mind was never to be deflected from it in even the slightest degree, by irrelevant considerations.

" Judge WORDEN's style of writing was strictly judicial. No one could express with more vigor and clearness, and in fewer words than he, precisely what he intended. He was never profuse or obscure; he never did, nor did he need to repeat a word.

" His thought and style were always direct and to the point. He was no sophist; he could not think or talk around and about a question. If he had anything to say, it was always to the point and full of meaning.

" This is not the time nor the place to discuss in detail the merits of the deceased's work. We can only say that its value is such that it has contributed, and will continue to contribute, largely to the stability of our institutions and the social wellbeing of our people.

" As a man Judge WORDEN was just and honorable. His

IN MEMORIAM.   607

tastes were refined; he was fond of music, and gave much of his time to general reading and culture. He loved his fellow men; his love of nature was strong; he loved the hills, the trees and everything that grew—he never saw a boulder without thinking of the immense period that had elapsed since the glacier began to move it southward. He was kind and amiable in disposition, generous in feeling, courteous in manners, and always, in the true sense of the word, a gentleman. There was, in his manners, his life and his methods of thought, a genial and pleasing simplicity. He never allowed his subject to overpower him. He always at last, however much time it might require, became the complete master of his subject. There was no sham, no pretence in the life or thought of this able man; nor could he tolerate these things in others.

"The deceased was a devoted and affectionate friend. The man that once secured his friendship, could not, if true to himself, be friendless.

"While the bar feel with peculiar force the great sorrow that has come to all, they are not without consolation.

"Their friend and brother, though not quite full of years, was full of honors and of good works; he was ripe for the harvest, and believing as he did, that 'He can't be wrong whose life is in the right,' he was ready and willing to meet the call of the Master. He passed away without pain, surrounded by wife, children and friends, and with the assurance that with him all would be well."

Zollars, C. J., in behalf of the court, responded as follows:

"Gentlemen of the Bar—No one more fully appreciated the worth of Judge Worden than the members of this court, and no one, aside from his immediate friends, could more keenly feel his loss. For many years he was a familiar figure about these halls, honored and respected by his associates for his honesty of purpose, soundness of judgment, and great learning as a judge. If any one ever questioned Judge Worden's judicial integrity, he knew not what manner of man he was. For more than forty years he was a resident of Indiana. For almost half of that time he was a member of this court. Added to this the time he served as prosecuting attorney and

608   IN MEMORIAM.

as circuit judge, the major part of his business life was spent in the public service. He came upon this bench in 1858, a young man, thirty-nine years of age. From his first opinion in the case of *Mills et al.* v. *The State, ex rel. Barbour et al.*, delivered in open court on the first day of the May term, 1858, and reported in the tenth volume of our reports at page 114, until his last opinion in the case of *The State* v. *Woodward*, filed on the second day of the November term, 1882, and reported in the eighty-ninth volume of the reports at page 110, he stood in the front ranks of the profession.

" Judge WORDEN'S work here is such as would adorn any bench in the land. He was a man of unusually strong common sense, and a clear, logical and discriminating mind. He was not a man of circumlocution, either in thought or word. There is a conciseness and directness of expression in his opinions that may well serve as a model to judges and lawyers. We shall offer no extended encomium upon his life or public service. By his work upon this bench, as embodied in his opinions extending over so many years, he erected his own monument, and wrote his own inscription. So long as Indiana shall be a Commonwealth, so long as its people shall have laws and courts, the name of Judge WORDEN will be known and honored. How much good he may have accomplished for the people of the State may never be noted or fully appreciated by the great mass of the people, but it will be, at least, by the profession and the more observing. It is altogether proper and becoming that this court, and the members of the bar of the State, should give public expression of their estimation and appreciation of the life, character and work of Judge WORDEN. It is just as proper also, that these proceedings shall go upon the records of this court, and be published in the reports, so that those not here, and those who shall come after us, may know that we, of his day and generation, respected and appreciated him in his life, and remembered and honored him in his death.

" It will be ordered, therefore, that these proceedings shall be spread upon the records of the court, and published in one of the reports."

Reprinted from B.R. Sulgrove. *History of Indianapolis and Marion County, Indiana*
(Philadelphia: L.H. Everts & Co., 1884), facing p. 200.

Thomas Andrews Hendricks

1819-1885

- Born September 7, 1819, near Zanesville, Ohio.

- Graduated in 1841 from Hanover College (Hanover, Indiana).

- Studied law with his uncle in Chambersburg, Pennsylvania.

- Admitted to the bar in 1843.

- Began first law practice in Shelbyville, Shelby County, Indiana.

- Elected as representative for Shelby County to the Indiana General Assembly in 1848.

- Served as a Democrat in the United States House of Representatives from 1851 to 1855.

- Ran unsuccessfully as a Democratic candidate for governor of Indiana in 1860.

- Elected to one term in the United States Senate in 1863.

Continued

Thomas Andrews Hendricks

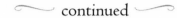 continued

---

- Elected governor of Indiana in 1872, serving from 1873 to 1876.

- Ran unsuccessfully for vice president of the United States in 1876.

- Elected vice president of the United States, under President Grover Cleveland, in 1885.

- Died suddenly November 25, 1885, in Indianapolis, Marion County, Indiana.

In Memoriam.

Comes now Hon. David Turpie, and presents the action taken at a meeting of the members of the Bar of this State, *in memoriam* of the life and character of Hon. THOMAS A. HENDRICKS, late Vice-President of the United States, and moves that these proceedings be entered upon the records of this court. The motion is granted, and the proceedings are now here entered of record as follows:

PROCEEDINGS

OF THE MEETING OF THE MEMBERS OF THE STATE BAR, HELD UPON THE OCCASION OF THE DEMISE OF THE LATE THOMAS A. HENDRICKS, VICE-PRESIDENT OF THE UNITED STATES.

Upon the 30th day of November, 1885, a very large number of the members of the Bar of the State of Indiana having met at 2 o'clock P. M., at the Federal Court-room in Indianapolis; present the Hon. William A. Woods, Judge of the United States District Court of the State of Indiana, and the other officers thereof.

The Hon. Solomon Claypool, addressing the court, moved that the Hon. W. Q. Gresham, Judge of the United States Circuit Court, act as chairman of the meeting, which motion prevailed.

Judge Gresham, in taking the chair, delivered a brief address upon the subject of the meeting, when, upon motion of W. H. H. Miller, Esq., William A. Ketcham, Esq., of the Indianapolis Bar, was chosen Secretary.

The Hon. David Turpie, chairman of the committee on

(601)

602   IN MEMORIAM.

resolutions, reported for consideration the following memorial annexed, as commemorative of the life, character and
public services of the deceased, and moved its adoption.

The motion was seconded by the Hon. Joseph E. McDonald, and after remarks by Messrs. Turpie, McDonald, Wil-
liamson, Frazer, Mack, Cravens, Coffroth and Love, and by
Judge Elliott, of the Supreme Court of the State, was unanimously carried.

Upon motion of Hon. Joseph E. McDonald, Hon. David
Turpie, chairman of the committee upon resolutions, was directed to present a copy thereof and of these proceedings for
record in the Circuit Court of the United States and the Supreme Court of the State, and the Secretary of the meeting
was directed to send a copy of the memorial and these proceedings to the family of the deceased.

The meeting then adjourned.

                                 W. Q. GRESHAM, *Chairman.*
W. A. KETCHAM, *Secretary.*

BAR MEMORIAL TO THOMAS A. HENDRICKS.

THOMAS A. HENDRICKS was born September 7th, 1819,
in Muskingum county, Ohio.   In 1820 his parents removed
to Indiana, first to Madison, then to Shelbyville, near which
they permanently resided.   His boyhood and youth were
spent in Shelby county on his father's farm.   They were
those of a pioneer, of an early settler in a sparsely populated
region, of what was then known elsewhere as the far West. His
life was thus, in every circumstance, coincident with the
morning of the State, the beginnings of civilization in a new
commonwealth.   Receiving at home a course of common
school education, he subsequently attended and graduated at
Hanover College, in Jefferson county.   Choosing the law as
a profession, he prosecuted his studies partly at Shelbyville,
partly at Chambersburgh, Pa., but was admitted to the bar
and commenced the practice at Shelbyville in 1843.   His
first public position was attained in 1848, by an election, un-

IN MEMORIAM. 603

solicited, to the House of Representatives of the General Assembly. Having served one term, and, declining further service therein, he was, in 1850, elected a member of the Constitutional Convention, being one of the youngest members of that body, and having in his associates many of the men most eminent in public life at that period.

In August, 1851, he was elected a representative in Congress and served two terms.

In August, 1855, he was tendered and accepted from President Pierce the position of Commissioner of the General Land-Office, at Washington, wherein he served nearly four years, resigning in the year 1859.

As the unanimous choice of his party, on the 12th day of January, 1863, he was elected a Senator of the United States for the term of six years, commencing on the 4th day of March, 1863, when he took his seat as such. He soon became in that distinguished body the recognized leader of his party, alike fitted for counsel and debate, endowed with that rare union of qualities, an equal proportion of caution and courage, so much needed in the conduct of a parliamentary opposition.

In 1872 he was elected Governor of Indiana, the first of his political party chosen to such a position after the close of the War, in any northern State. As Governor he originated the system of making and preserving in that department a permanent record of executive action upon all applications before him. His administration was distinguished for more than ordinary attention to the cause of popular education, for the humane appeals by the executive in behalf of the benevolent institutions of the State, appeals which met a response from the General Assembly alike creditable to themselves and their constituents.

In 1877, and again in 1884, he visited Europe, travelling through the British islands and the principal countries of the continent. A single remark made upon his return from his first tour, "that the French were a people much attached to their country, not at all to their institutions of government,"

604   IN MEMORIAM.

shows the habit of thoughtful observation which characterized even his leisure.

In 1884 he was elected Vice-President of the United States,
and entered upon his duties as such on the 4th day of March,
1885, serving as the presiding officer of the Senate during
the brief executive session held under the new administration.

From the farm-house to the Vice-Presidency—such was
the commencement and end of a career untouched by dis-
honor, unclouded by suspicion. His public acts as a Senator and Representative in Congress have gone into history.
His record has received the highest possible commendation
and approval from the vast constituency he served, by his
subsequent preferment to the second office in the gift of the
Nation—from the consideration, also, that begun in one age,
his countrymen of another generation arose to do him honor
and to complete the full-orbed cycle of his fame.

Mr. Hendricks was, throughout the whole period of his
active life, a lawyer, even in his last days concerned in the
conduct of causes. His entrance upon and employments in
public life were episodes, excursions useful to himself and
others, but did not divert him from the beaten path of forensic labor. On the floor of the Senate, in the halls of legislation, he sojourned; at the bar, in the courts, he dwelt.
He was engaged in very much of the important litigation at
the capital of his State. His practice was by no means local.
He attended, in the discharge of his professional duties,
nearly every circuit in our own, and many of the higher
courts of adjoining States and the Supreme Court at Washington. Much of his life, however, was non-professional.
His time and thought were, at very frequently recurring in-
tervals, given to the work of the hustings. There was something in the mere aspect of a large popular assembly which
had for him a special attraction. His manner in addressing
a mixed audience was peculiarly his own—neither that of
conversation nor oratory; something better suited than either
to his purpose. He was one of the most impressive and successful of public canvassers. Nor did he disregard the un-
considered trifles of the campaign. There was an affluent

IN MEMORIAM. 605

grace in his salutations which largely supplemented argument. He was, moreover, a man of normal action and opinion, following the ordinary bent and tenets of his party; no fanatic, zealot, or extremist upon any subject, not such a one as the multitude often follow, but a character smoothly rounded to completeness, without edges or angles, with no corners in his creed political; yet he was and continued to be a popular favorite to the last.

To the stores of information acquired by extensive travel and intercourse, both at home and abroad, he added a close acquaintance with the works of the best authors, being a careful habitual reader of books, not less than of men. His literary taste was highly cultivated. His excellence as a writer, manifest enough in his messages and state papers, would have earned particular recognition, but that it had been overshadowed by his more imposing reputation as a public speaker.

In religion he was an Episcopalian, an active member and officer for many years of St. Paul's Church, Indianapolis. Upon this subject he was firm in his conviction, in his life consistent, in his Christian profession unobtrusive. He walked with humility in faith. A man much given to charity, and of the most enlightened and liberal tolerance; nevertheless, he was strongly attached to his church, to his party, to his State, giving voice often with emphasis to his affection, that men might note not him but these, the so greatly revered objects of his devotion and regard.

The virtues of his private life were such as may be most commended in the friend, the neighbor, and the citizen. He was naturally of a disposition sedate, though cheerful; in address urbane; in manner extremely affable, but with dignity; in conversation pleasing; in society attracting, but not engrossing, the attention of others; to woman deferential with a high degree of courtesy unforced, indicative of respect and interest. Such was Hendricks.

Discerning the man, his life and acts at large, in the mass, in that respect, too, most nearly concerning ourselves, we may say, with verity, he was pre-eminently a product of Indiana,

606   IN MEMORIAM.

an offspring of the State, a growth of its laws and institutions, and that the just pride taken in him by the people of
this commonwealth was entertained not without reason for a
fellow-citizen so illustrious.

He died in this city, where he would have wished to die,
where he most really lived, at home, surrounded by those
whom he loved; in the metropolis of the State which he had
served so long, and by which he had been so often and so
highly honored.   Not without unavailing sorrow for a calamity so grievous, do we tender to his bereaved consort and the
kindred of his household, our profound condolence and sin-
cerest sympathy in the irreparable loss which has befallen
them.

DAVID TURPIE,
A. L. ROACHE,
A. C. HARRIS,
NOBLE C. BUTLER,
CHAS. L. HOLSTEIN,
H. D. PIERCE, *Sec'y.*   *Bar Memorial Committee.*

Mr. Turpie also moved that an order be made directing
that the proceedings herein above set forth be published with
the reported decisions of this court and as a part of its official
proceedings.

To this motion Chief Justice NIBLACK, on behalf of the
court, responded as follows:

" It has not been the custom of this court to cause the proceedings taken by the Bar of the State upon the death of
any of its members, however distinguished, to be published
with the reports of its decisions, unless the person in
whose memory the proceedings were held, at the time
of his death, or at some previous time, had some official
connection with the court.   The precedent which has been
thus observed is one which we think ought not to be departed from except in a strongly exceptional case.

" Mr. Hendricks was, for more than a third of a century, a
practicing attorney of this court, distinguished alike for his
high personal character and for his professional ability.

IN MEMORIAM. 607

Having, in addition, filled the highest official positions which the State could confer upon him, as well as places of high trust under the national government, and having been Vice-President of the United States at the time of his death, we regard the proceedings now before us as of much more than ordinary interest to the legal profession and to the public generally. The case presented is one in which an eminent lawyer and an honored member of this Bar had well nigh reached the highest official distinction known to our form of government. We, consequently, feel justified in treating the occasion as a strongly exceptional one, and in directing that the proceedings be published, as requested, with our reported decisions.

"It is accordingly so ordered."

Joseph A. S. Mitchell
1837-1890

- Born December 21, 1837, near Mercersburg, Pennsylvania.
- Moved to Illinois at the age of seventeen to attend Blandisville Academy for three years.
- Studied law in Chambersburg, Pennsylvania, in 1856.
- Admitted to the Indiana bar in 1859.
- Opened a law office in Goshen, Elkhart County, Indiana, in 1860.
- Enlisted in the Union Army at the beginning of the Civil War, serving in the cavalry for two years.
- Re-entered legal practice in Goshen, forming a partnership with Judge John H. Baker.
- Elected to two terms as mayor of Goshen, serving from 1872 to 1874.
- Served on the board of trustees for DePauw University (Greencastle, Indiana).
- Elected to the Indiana Supreme Court in 1884, serving from January 6, 1885, until his death.
- Died December 12, 1890, in Goshen, Elkhart County, Indiana.

In Memoriam.

At a meeting of the Indianapolis Bar, held on Saturday, the 13th day of December, 1890, Byron K. Elliott, Addison C. Harris, Frederick Rand, William A. Ketcham, and John A. Holman were appointed a committee to prepare a memorial and resolutions expressive of the respect of the members of the bar for the life and character of Judge JOSEPH A. S. MITCHELL, and of their sorrow for his death. The committee reported the following memorial and resolutions, which were unanimously adopted:

MEMOIR.

JOSEPH A. S. MITCHELL was born near Mercersburg, Franklin county, Pennsylvania, December 21, 1837. His father died while he was a child, and he was left to make his own way through the world, which, as his career shows, he did manfully. In his seventeenth year he entered Blandenville Academy, in Illinois, where he devoted himself to his studies with that zeal and industry which have been so conspicuously characteristic of his manhood's years. At the end of three years he was graduated, and for one term was a teacher in the institution from which he received his diploma. He spent the next two years in the study of the law at Chambersburg, Pennsylvania, and subsequently came to Goshen, in this State. In 1865, he married Miss Mary E. Defrees, a lady richly gifted with intellectual and social qualities. She and two children, a daughter and son, survive him. For more than a quarter of a century the city of Goshen has been his home; there he has lived, honored and respected, as few men have ever been, by his townsmen; there he died, on the morning of Friday, the 12th day of

(601)

602 ## IN MEMORIAM.

December, 1890, mourned not only by his neighbors and townsmen, but also by the people of a great State.

In 1860 he began the practice of his profession, and a bright prospect opened before him, but he continued in practice only until the spring of 1861, when he cast aside his books and his business to become a soldier in the army of the Union. He was in many battles, in many long and weary marches, and in many perilous military enterprises. In them all he was a gallant soldier and a true gentleman, winning respect from his comrades and praise from his officers. He left the service with the rank of captain, a rank, as the events of his later life conclusively show, much below his merit and capacity; but so great was his modesty, and so little was he inclined to secure advancement by exalting his own merits, that, to those who knew him well, it is no marvel that he did not reach a higher military rank.

At the expiration of the term of his service he returned to Goshen, and, entering into partnership with Hon. John H. Baker, resumed the practice of the law. He commanded success at the bar, and rose rapidly to eminence, for he was a vigorous reasoner, a learned lawyer, and a sagacious advocate. He was honored by the State Bar Association by being chosen as one of its representatives to the convention at Saratoga, in 1879; his colleagues were Benjamin Harrison and Azro Dyer. In 1880 his party nominated him for the office of Judge of the Supreme Court of the State, but, in common with the other candidates of his party, he was defeated. In 1884 he was a successful candidate, and in November last was elected for a second time. Death struck him down while yet serving his first term; upon his second he will never enter. The first term was productive of rich fruitage; but, with his judgment ripened by experience, and his mental powers trained by discipline, the fruitage of the second term, could he have been spared to fill it, would have been still greater and richer.

Of JOSEPH A. S. MITCHELL it may be written, with strict truth, that he was a just judge, and of no man can greater praise be truthfully spoken. He possessed, in an eminent

IN MEMORIAM.   603

degree, the qualifications of a judge ; he was upright and impartial, courteous and patient, learned and able.   His morality was of the highest type ; pure things he loved, impure ones he despised.   His conceptions of the principles of justice were clear, his adherence to them courageous and manful.   His judgments were formed with care, and expressed with vigor.   He explored the authorities with diligence ; he studied the reasoning of the great judges of England and America with singular discernment, and he sought the principles of right and justice with zealous care.   His keen discrimination, his masterful analytical power, and his logical methods of thought enabled him to grasp with strength and apply with wisdom the principles of jurisprudence.   His judicial opinions are of massive strength, and their language is clear and forcible.   In all the States of the Union his opinions command respect, and his rank as a jurist is high. His opinions will be studied as long as our Reports exist, for judgments so sound and reasoning so clear are for all time.

The private character and life of Judge MITCHELL were without stain.   A man of deep religious convictions, and ardent in his attachment to his church, he was too liberal to be a bigot, and too just to be intolerant.   His religious professions he made good by his conduct ; he lived unspotted and faithful to his creed.   His courtesy and kindness were unfailing.   Arguments he heard with patience, and weighed with care.   In debate he contended stoutly for his own convictions, but with chivalric courtesy.   A contest did not arouse him to anger, nor the heat of debate provoke him to bitter words.   Arguments he used with power, epithets he disdained.   When such a man dies it becomes men to mourn.

Resolved, That in the death of Judge MITCHELL the State has lost a judge fitted by temperament, by learning, and by the highest attributes of moral character for the position he has filled with such high honor to the State, and such great credit to himself and to the profession he loved so well ; and that we deplore his death, not only because of his great

604 IN MEMORIAM.

worth as a man and a citizen, but also because of his loss to
the judiciary of the Commonwealth of which he was an honored and useful member.

Resolved, That we present to the family of the departed
Judge our sincere sympathy and condolence in their bereavment.

Resolved, That the Secretary be requested to transmit a
copy of this Memoir and these resolutions to the family of
our deceased brother.

Resolved, That this Memoir and these resolutions be presented to the Supreme Court of the State, and to the United
States Circuit Court, for such action as may be fit and appropriate, and that a committee be appointed for that purpose.

ADDRESS OF MR. ADDISON C. HARRIS, PRESENTING THE MEMORIAL AND RESOLUTIONS.

MAY IT PLEASE THE COURT:—I rise to present the
memorial and resolutions of the Bar in commemoration of
the life and character of the late Judge JOSEPH A. S.
MITCHELL. These are so full and expressive that no more
is needed on the part of the Bar as a tribute to his memory,
and yet I am impelled, in their behalf, to speak a word concerning his career upon this bench.

To sit in judgment over all in the State, is the highest
trust which the people can confer upon any man. To this
bench it is given not only to decide questions of law arising
between men, but it is made the arbiter of many questions arising between the co-ordinate departments of the
State. Under the Constitution this great court is the umpire, empowered to draw the line of constitutional right between the legislative and executive departments of this commonwealth. At no time, during the history of the State,
have more questions, or questions deeper, or more far-reach-

IN MEMORIAM.   605

ing in their consequences, been decided than during the period in which Judge MITCHELL sat on this bench. Cases like
these call for the exercise of the most careful reasoning, of
the keenest penetration and forecast. They spring out of the
Constitution, and must be measured on, and decided by, the
true principles of republican government.

All minds have never been quite in harmony as to the precise fundamentals of our system of government. From the
birth of the republic statesmen and jurists have given their
best thoughts to, and debated these questions with the warmth
and zeal which always come of earnest and settled conviction. Thus did Judge MITCHELL. With his mature and de-
liberate convictions as a basis, he analyzed these cases with
his rare powers of research and reason, reaching and declaring his conclusions so frankly, and with arguments so forcible, and at once so entirely indifferent to the immediate consequences, that all men accorded him the respect which integrity of purpose ever commands.

His powers were given unreservedly to the course of jurisprudence. He never sought to discover new rules of law,
but rather aimed to master and intelligently apply the established canons of the law. Thoughtful, deliberative, firm in
his convictions, he was yet eager to hear, and listened to
every counsel with the same interest and attention.

To these qualities, it must be added, that he held, in a
rare manner, to use the words of Cicero, "affability in hearing, calmness in determining, and carefulness in deciding
the case."

He felt, as all judges must feel whose words are preserved,
that the importance of the case was not so much to the parties themselves as to the entire people, whose future conduct
and rights were to be measured by the reason and words of
the opinion.

The greatest purpose of a court of last resort is not to decide cases by numbers, but rather by its decisions to lay
down accurately and in plain words, the rule whereby the
people may thereafter guide their conduct in similar transactions, and have and hold their rights by mutual accord,

606 IN MEMORIAM.

without room for misunderstanding as to their rights under the law.

The clearness and conciseness of the opinions of Judge MITCHELL, from his first case to his last, indicate that this thought was never absent from his mind ; and while he was not permitted, under the providence of God, to continue a member of this tribunal as long as some, both living and dead, yet the impress his thought has made upon the judicature and laws of the Commonwealth will endure as long as our State shall live.

" There is one universal law, which commands that one shall be born, and shall die."

May every one submit as calmly to the final decree as your late brother. With a noble regard for the memory of one of your number, now no more, in behalf of the Bar, I move that the memorial and resolutions be spread upon the record of this court as a truthful testimonial of his life and worth.

MR. CHIEF JUSTICE OLDS REPLIED AS FOLLOWS.

The court receives the resolutions adopted by the Bar, in relation to the death of the late Justice MITCHELL, and the remarks of the Hon. A. C. Harris in presenting them, with deep regret for the loss of the member of this court to whom they relate. They are no more than are due to the occasion.

Justice MITCHELL came to the bench in the prime of life, fortified for his work by years of experience and training in the law, and the ways of the courts, acquired as a successful practitioner at the bar. Being possessed of a mind well stored with general as well as legal knowledge, with energy, force of character, and firm in his determinations, he was well fitted for judicial duties. He had the energy to investigate, the ability to grasp and comprehend important questions, and to discriminate and reject illogical theories. When he arrived at a conclusion and formed an opinion he stood firmly by it, and maintained his position with ability in well reasoned and clearly expressed opinions. The results of his labors upon this bench are in the volumes of the Reports of the decisions of this court, commencing with the 99th of Indiana. In the decisions delivered by him will be found the evidence of his industry and ability as a judge. His style was vigorous and clear. How well he did his work, and with what ability, the decisions delivered by him will speak and be felt as establishing rules of law long after commendatory resolutions and addresses, of whatever character, are forgotten. As a man, he was endowed by nature with qualities making him steadfast and firm in action, and kind and courteous toward all with whom his action brought him in contact.

Being in the prime of life, and having been in apparent good health, the news of his death carried with it unusual gloom and sorrow.

The resolutions of the Bar, just presented to us, with the remarks of the Hon. A. C. Harris, will be placed upon the records of the court.

It is further ordered that all proceedings in relation to the death of the late Justice MITCHELL, which have been received by the clerk, be placed on the files of the court.

John Griffith Berkshire
1832-1891

- Born in 1832 in Ohio County, Indiana.

- Educated in Rising Sun, Ohio County, Indiana.

- Studied law at Asbury University (now known as DePauw University) in Greencastle, Putnam County, Indiana, graduating in 1857.

- Opened a law office in Versailles, Ripley County, Indiana, in 1857.

- Served as judge of the First and Sixth Indiana Judicial Circuits from 1864 to 1882.

- Moved to North Vernon, Jennings County, Indiana, after losing his bid for re-election in 1882, and opened a private legal practice.

- Elected to the Indiana Supreme Court in 1888, serving from January 17, 1889, until his death.

- Died February 19, 1891, in North Vernon, Jennings County, Indiana.

In Memoriam.

Judge JOHN GRIFFITH BERKSHIRE was born in Millersburgh, Kentucky, on the 12th day of November, 1832. When a child he removed, with his father, to Indiana. At the early age of ten years he began the trade of blacksmith, in the shop with his father. His early education was wholly confined to the common schools of the State. In the year 1856 he entered law school at Asbury University, and was graduated in 1857. Soon after receiving his diploma he entered upon the practice of his chosen profession at Versailles, Indiana, and by his legal learning, industry, and strict attention to the interests of his clients soon acquired a lucrative practice. In the year 1861 he married Miss Gussie Clendening, a lady of rare attainments, who survives him. He had, by her, two children, one of whom, a married daughter, is still living.

He was nominated by the Republicans for the office of circuit judge, for the circuit composed of the counties of Jefferson, Switzerland, Ohio, Ripley, Jennings, Bartholomew, and Brown, in the year 1864, and was elected. He was renominated, by acclamation, for the same position in the years 1870 and 1876, and was elected, serving his constituents in the capacity of circuit judge for the period of eighteen years.

In 1882 he was nominated by the Republican State Convention for the office of Judge of the Supreme Court, but was defeated, with his party, at the ensuing election. In 1888, he was again nominated, by acclamation, for the same office, and was elected.

In all his undertakings he brought to bear intelligent method, and untiring energy and industry. Though not a member of any church organization, he was a firm believer in the Christian religion, and a generous supporter of the

(601)

602   IN MEMORIAM.

Methodist church.   His private character was without blem-
ish, and his voice was always heard on the side of morality.
He was frank, kind-hearted, and courteous, generous to a
fault; a firm friend, and a kind and loving husband and father.   As a judge, he had few equals.   In the administration of the law he brought to bear the same method, energy,
and industry that characterized all his conduct through life.
He was a sound lawyer, patient in research, broad and comprehensive in his views, conscientious, upright, and fearless.
His opinions, while on the supreme bench, constitute a monument of which the bar of the State may well be proud.

On the evening of the 19th day of February, 1891, he died
at his home, in North Vernon, Indiana, surrounded by family
and friends.   In the death of such men the community loses
its most valued public servants, and the State its brightest
jewels.

Resolved, That in the death of Judge BERKSHIRE the
State has lost a judge fitted by temperament, by learning,
and by the highest attributes of moral character for the position he has filled with such high honor to the State, and
such great credit to himself, and to the profession he loved;
and that we deplore his death, not only because of his great
worth as a man and a citizen, but also because of his loss to
the judiciary of the commonwealth, of which he was an honored and useful member.

Resolved, That we present to the family of the departed
Judge our sincere sympathy and condolence in their bereavement.

Resolved, That the Secretary be requested to transmit a
copy of this Memoir, and these resolutions, to the family of
the deceased.

Resolved, That this Memoir and these resolutions be presented to the Supreme Court, and to the United States Circuit Court, for such action as may be fit and appropriate, and
that a committee be appointed for that purpose.

Filed April 2, 1891.

IN MEMORIAM.   603

MAY IT PLEASE THE COURT :—The Hon. JOHN G. BERK-
SHIRE, one of the members of this court, departed this life
at his home in North Vernon, Indiana, on the evening of
the 19th day of February, A. D. 1891. In view of this
sad and unexpected event, a largely attended meeting of the
members of the bar of the State was held at the Supreme
Court room, in the State-house, on the 21st day of February, A. D. 1891, and a memorial and resolutions were
adopted.

By a resolution passed at the meeting, it was made our
duty to present the memorial and resolutions to this court,
and ask that they be spread upon its records.

They give a brief outline of Judge BERKSHIRE's private
and official life, and express the high appreciation of the
members of the profession, for his character and public
services. It was our fortune to know Judge BERKSHIRE,
intimately, from his early manhood, and to know the adverse surroundings of his early life, through which he strug-
gled up to an honorable and useful career.

He was a man of strong and positive convictions, and of
active, earnest and persistent effort, seeking to know the
right and pursuing it with unswerving purpose.

We move the court that the memorial and resolutions be
spread upon its record.   ROBERT N. LAMB.
                                             RALPH HILL.
                                             F. WINTER.

REPLY OF MR. CHIEF JUSTICE OLDS.

Mr. Chief Justice OLDS replied as follows : The court
receives the resolutions of the Bar in regard to the death of
the late Justice BERKSHIRE, and the address of the gentlemen of the committee, the Hon. Robert N. Lamb, Hon. F.
Winter and Hon. Ralph Hill, in presenting them, with a
deep sensibility of the worth of the late Justice as a citizen
and jurist. We fully appreciate the great loss sustained by
the State and the bar in his death. The loss is most keenly

604 IN MEMORIAM.

felt by the members of this court who were associated with him. They were impressed by his pure instincts, his open, frank and honest traits of character, with his ability and learning and his unswerving integrity as a jurist. By these noble traits of character which he possessed we were not only induced to respect and admire him as a jurist, but we became attached to him as a friend. While he was a man of positive character, and fearless to express, and able to maintain with signal ability his views on all important questions, he was as kind-hearted as a child.

In regard to his worth as a citizen, and his work as a jurist, we most heartily concur in all that has been said in the memorial and the address of the committee.

The result of his labors as a justice of this court are to be seen in the volumes of the reports of the decisions of the court from the 117th to the 126th of Indiana inclusive. The decisions delivered by him while a member of this court are evidence of his industry, and they will stand as a monument to his memory and speak as to his ability as a judge long after what may have been said of him in way of comment during his life or tributes to his memory at his death has been forgotten.

Having a clear conception of the law, his style of expression was vigorous and clear. He sought to base his opinions on some well-founded and established principles of law rather than to follow a case on account of its having some elements of similarity with the one being considered.

Possessed of a broad comprehensive mind, and having years of experience on the circuit bench, he entered upon his duties as a member of this court well qualified to render valuable services to the State, and we believe he fully met the expectations of all while he remained here. Having served only about one-third of the time for which he was elected it is reasonable to suppose that had he lived during the last years of his services he would have builded even a greater monument to his memory as a jurist, but his life and his work have ended.

IN MEMORIAM.   605

The resolutions of the Bar just presented to us, with the address of the committee, will be placed upon the records of the court.

It is further ordered that any other resolutions presented be filed by the clerk of this court.

Filed April 2, 1891.

William Ellis Niblack

1822-1893

- Born May 19, 1822, in Dubois County, Indiana.

- Attended a log school until age sixteen, when he entered Indiana University in 1838.

- Failed to graduate from Indiana University due to father's death.

- Worked as a surveyor while studying law.

- Began practicing law in Dover Hill, Martin County, Indiana, in 1845.

- Elected numerous times to both the House of Representatives and the Senate of the Indiana General Assembly, serving from 1849 to 1852 and from 1863 to 1864.

- Appointed judge of the Third Circuit Court in 1854.

- Served in the United States House of Representatives from 1857 to 1861 and from 1865 to 1875.

Continued

William Ellis Niblack

 continued

- Participated actively in national Democratic politics.

- Served on the Indiana Supreme Court from January 1, 1877, until January 7, 1889.

- Died May 4, 1893, in Indianapolis, Marion County, Indiana.

In Memoriam.

MEETING OF THE STATE BAR ASSOCIATION COMMEMORATING THE DEATH OF HON. WM. E. NIBLACK, HELD IN SUPREME COURT ROOM MAY 9TH, 1893.

The meeting was called to order by Mr. Silas M. Shepard, attorney. On motion, Hon. Silas D. Coffey, C. J. Supreme Court, was chosen chairman, and Andrew M. Sweeney, secretary. The committee on memorial, consisting of Hons. Byron K. Elliott, A. L. Roach, F. Rand, S. Claypool and Noble C. Butler, clerk United States Court, reported a fitting memorial upon the life and distinguished services of JUDGE NIBLACK. The report was unanimously adopted.

Eulogiums were pronounced by Hon. Addison C. Harris, Hon. John L. Griffiths, Hon. Chas. Cox, Hon. Caleb S. Denny, and Ex-United States Attorney-General W. H. H. Miller, of Indianapolis, and by Hon. David C. Gooding, of Greenfield.

On motion, the secretary was instructed to send copies of the memorial to the Circuit, Superior, the United States, the Supreme Court, and the Knox Circuit Court, to be spread upon their records. A copy was also ordered sent to the widow.

The meeting then adjourned.

S. D. COFFEY, Chairman.
A. M. SWEENEY, Sec'y.

MEMORIAL.

WILLIAM ELLIS NIBLACK was born in Dubois county, Indiana, on the 19th day of May, 1822. He was one of seven children, and while his parents had a fair share of worldly goods, for the community in which they lived at

(702)

the time of his birth and during his youth and early
manhood, they were unable to furnish him with any
more than what would now be regarded as very limited
educational advantages.   His services were needed on
the farm and in the mill and tannery of his father, and
were cheerfully and faithfully rendered.   But these
duties did not prevent his obtaining a sufficient amount
of schooling to enable him to enter the university at
Bloomington, when he was about fifteen years of age.
The death of his father, when young NIBLACK was in his
sixteenth year, abruptly terminated his collegiate life
and made it necessary for him, as the eldest son in the
bereaved family, to return home and devote himself to
their maintenance.   He worked on the farm and taught
school, and managed a trading boat, and assisted the surveyor of his county in the discharge of the duties of that
office.   He was ready for any work that promised an immediate support for the family, and he engaged in it
with ardor and industry.   At the same time he secretly
desired and thought he had discovered in the law a
broader field for the exercise of his powers, and embraced
every opportunity to equip himself for the practice of it.
His success was such that by the time he had attained
his twenty-first year he was admitted to the bar and began the practice of law at Dover Hill, in Martin county.
He soon became a leader among the citizens of that
county and the neighboring one of Daviess, who availed
themselves of his abilities by making him, in 1849, their
representative in the Legislature of the State, where he
served them for three years.   In 1850, he was selected
by the same constituency to represent it in the Senate of
Indiana.   He was appointed by the Governor, in 1854,
judge of a circuit comprising sixteen of the counties in
the southwestern part of the State, and under this appointment served out the unexpired term of Alvin P.
Hovey, and at the expiration of it was elected for another

704 IN MEMORIAM.

term. He removed to Vincennes in 1855, and in the following year his judicial career was interrupted by his election to Congress. He represented the Vincennes district in Congress until the war, when he voluntarily yielded the position to John Law, who held it for the next four years. At the close of that period MR. NIBLACK, who had in the meantime served another term in the State Legislature, was returned to Congress, and served continuously until 1876. After leaving the halls of Congress he was elected one of the judges of our Supreme Court, and served in that capacity for a period of twelve years. At the close of his judicial service, in 1888, he removed to Indianapolis, where he engaged in the practice of law, and remained until his death, on the 7th day of May, 1893.

His inheritance of Scotch-Irish blood, and the conditions of his birth and early life, combined to make a positive and resolute character. He met and overcame the difficulties of life by earnest and persistent effort, and sheer force and tenacity of purpose. Reverses of fortune never soured or embittered him. Towards his associates and acquaintances he was always one of the kindest and most considerate of men. He took a benevolent interest in all his fellow-creatures. His fund of human sympathy was exhaustless and increased with the numerous drafts upon it. It was natural and sincere, and attracted and bound men to him. He made for himself in public life a name and reputation which extended beyond the limits of his own State, and he had among his friends some of the most eminent men of our country, in both of the great political parties. He never confined his friendship to any one of them, or

"Gave up to party what was meant for mankind."

He was distinguished as a statesman by his breadth and liberality of view. He was broadened and ripened

for his duties as a judge by his political experience, and
his insight into human affairs was enlarged and deep-
ened by it. He had none of the pedantry of his profession, and cared little for its technicalities. His opinions were announced in plain and perspicuous language,
and were easily intelligible to others, beause he always
understood himself. His moral and. intellectual per-
ceptions were clear and accurate, and his sense of justice,
of fairness, and of equity, was almost infallible. He had a
firm grasp of fundamental principles, and the faculty for
applying them. He had the respect and confidence of
the bar at all times, and was regarded by it as an able
and upright judge. It deplores his death as a serious
loss to the legal profession and the State, into whose
history his life entered as an important factor, and
whose interests were promoted by it in every way.

BYRON K. ELLIOTT.

A. L. ROACH.

F. RAND.

S. CLAYPOOL.

NOBLE C. BUTLER,

Committee.

Filed May 9, 1893.

Image courtesy of Manuscript Section, Indiana State Library.

Walter Quinton Gresham
~ 1832-1895 ~

- Born March 17, 1832, near Lanesville, Harrison County, Indiana.

- Attended Indiana University, but left before graduating.

- Studied law at Corydon, Harrison County, Indiana, and admitted to the bar in 1854.

- Elected as a Republican to the Indiana House of Representatives in 1860.

- Enlisted in the 38th Regiment, Indiana Volunteer Infantry in 1861.

- Advanced to colonel of the 53rd Regiment, Indiana Volunteer Infantry in 1862.

- Mustered out of the Army as a major general in 1865 due to wounds sustained during the Atlanta campaign.

Continued ~

Walter Quinton Gresham

 continued

- Worked in New York City as a financial agent for Indiana from 1867 to 1868.

- Appointed to the United States Circuit Court for the district of Indiana by President Ulysses S. Grant on September 1, 1869, serving until 1883.

- Appointed United States Postmaster General by President Arthur in 1883.

- Accepted appointment as judge of the Seventh Judicial Circuit in 1884, serving until March 6, 1893.

- Lost the Republican nomination for president of the United States to Benjamin Harrison, causing him to shift his political allegiances to the Democratic Party.

- Appointed secretary of state by President Grover Cleveland, serving from 1893 until his death.

- Died May 28, 1895, in Washington, D.C.

In Memoriam.

WALTER Q. GRESHAM.

At a meeting of the bar of Marion county, Indiana, held in the United States Circuit Court room, at Indianapolis, May 31, 1895, the following memorial on the death of WALTER Q. GRESHAM was reported by the committee and unanimously adopted:

"WALTER Q. GRESHAM died in Washington on the morning of May 28, A. D. 1895. He was born in Indiana, and lived the longer part of his life in this State, and was well known throughout the country.

"By the force of his abilities he rose step by step in the esteem of the people, and during his long and useful life served the State and Nation well as lawyer, legislator, soldier, judge and statesman.

"Appointed to the federal bench, he took his seat on the first day of September, 1869. Here he resided for nearly twenty-three years. It was a time when the duties were many, arduous, and often difficult to perform.

"His executive ability, combined with his deep sense of right and devotion to impartial justice, enabled him, day by day, to take up every judicial duty as it came to hand and discharge it promptly, fairly, and impartially.

"During his long judicial career it was his custom to take a practical rather than a theoretical or philosophical view of all affairs, whether small or great, that came before him for consideration and judgment. In this way he was enabled to dispose of the great volume of varied business that was constantly pressing upon him for hearing.

"His loyalty to the Nation, his achievements and

(706)

sacrifices on the field of battle and his services in the
councils of the cabinet are written in the history of the
Republic.

"These are but part of his generous and noble character.   It was as a judge in this court that the bench and
bar, intimately associated with him, learned to know
and appreciate the nobility of his life.   Conscience was
his guide.   To do the right, as God gave him to see the
right, was the pure light by which he reached his conclusions.   These conclusions are recorded upon the im-
perishable rolls of this court.   They tell the story of his
integrity of purpose and deep and abiding love of equal
and impartial justice; and we, who are still living, desire to enroll upon these records our tribute to his memory.   He was a just judge."

Resolved, That the secretary of this meeting present to
and cause this memorial to be spread upon the record of
the Supreme Court of Indiana, the United States courts
for the district of Indiana and the superior and circuit
courts of Marion county, Indiana.

A. C. HARRIS,

JOHN T. DYE,

FRANK B. BURKE,

LAWSON M. HARVEY,

NOBLE C. BUTLER,

Committee.

Witness our hands as Chairman and Secretary of said
meeting.

JOHN H. BAKER,

Chairman.

PLINY W. BARTHOLOMEW,

Secretary.

Filed June 13, 1895.

Reprinted from B.R. Sulgrove. *History of Indianapolis and Marion County, Indiana*
(Philadelphia: L.H. Everts & Co., 1884), facing p. 204.

John Maynard Butler

1834-1882

- Born September 17, 1834, in Evansville, Vanderburgh County, Indiana.

- Graduated from Wabash College (Crawfordsville, Indiana) in 1856.

- Accepted the job as president of the Female Seminary at Crawfordsville, Montgomery County, Indiana, promptly after graduation.

- Became high school principal in Crawfordsville and began studying law in 1859.

- Started practicing law in 1861 and quickly became known as one of the more successful lawyers in the state of Indiana.

- Moved to Indianapolis, Marion County, Indiana, in 1871, forming the law firm of McDonald, Butler & Mason with Joseph E. McDonald and A.L. Mason.

- Died November 10, 1882.

In Memoriam.

JOHN M. BUTLER.

Memorial of the bar of Indiana, on the death of JOHN M. BUTLER, Esq., unanimously adopted September 18, 1895, at the Federal court room in Indianapolis.

Hon. BENJAMIN HARRISON, President.
LINTON A. COX, Esq., Secretary.

In the death of JOHN M. BUTLER, at the age of 61 years, the bar of the city, the State and the Nation has suffered a notable loss.

The son of a Presbyterian minister, reared amid the privations incident to life in a pioneer minister's family in Indiana 60 years ago, JOHN M. BUTLER was fortunate in the time, the place and the circumstances of his nativity. The timbre of his mind and soul was of a fiber to grow stronger, rather than break in a struggle with the currents of adverse environment.

Endowed by nature with an intellect of great vigor, backed by an aggressive and unbending will, in the school of poverty he was perforce driven to habits of industry, of self-reliance and frugality, which were main elements of his notable professional success, and which ended only with his life.

As a rule men, like horses, do their best only under the whip and spur, and he is the fortunate boy and youth and young man who has necessity for a driver.

Mr. BUTLER was also fortunate in the circumstances of his early professional life. He traveled the circuit from county to county, compelled to be ready and to try causes with little opportunity to consult libraries, and thus acquired the habit, much more common a generation ago

(708)

IN MEMORIAM. 709

than now, of reliance upon principles rather than precedents.

Mr. BUTLER was very thorough in the preparation of his cases,—never forgetting that his clients were entitled to his best service.

He was very methodical,—well knowing that the details of a large practice at the bar can only be kept in hand by rigid system.

He was as good a type of the lawyer of to-day as contrasted with the lawyer of the date of his birth, as the country affords.

Three-quarters of a century ago trials, not only before juries, but even in that most august tribunal, the Supreme Court of the United States, were contests of eloquence,—forensic battles, where orators, like Pinkney and Wirt, clothed their arguments in the most ornate and elaborate rhetoric.

To-day such efforts are not only not made,—they are not attempted or even expected. In that court the lawyer is in best repute, and is most effective, who has the facts and the law of his case best in hand and who most simply and most directly presents them to the court; and such, in a very large measure, is the rule everywhere. The profession of the law has become, very largely, a system of business management, and the lawyer most sought after is he who is not merely a trier of law suits, but a prudent and wise business adviser.

Such a lawyer was Mr. BUTLER. He was a very capable business man, and he was a very practical and effective trial lawyer. He did not assume to be an orator. He lacked the fancy, the imagination, sense of humor, the ever ready springs of feeling necessary for an orator.

He had, however, qualities more useful to his clients and more effective in his profession in these times,—a logic as inexorable as political economy, and a direct-

710   IN MEMORIAM.

ness, terseness and force of speech rarely equaled. With him law was logic, and logic was law.

Mr. BUTLER was not uncharitable, yet he was essentially a partisan. His convictions on most subjects were strong, not infrequently radical. Having such convictions, it was natural that a courageous man should express them fearlessly and plainly, and Mr. BUTLER was a man of courage.

He always made his client's cause his own; put himself in his place. He was always an agreeable and welcome associate, and a respected but dangerous opponent.

No member of the Indiana bar has achieved a greater professional success than he whose death we mourn today. The death of no lawyer in Indiana, and of few in the country, would leave a wider gap in the profession.

JOHN M. BUTLER was a good friend, a good neighbor, a good citizen, and a good man.

Therefore, we, his brethren in his chosen profession, beg to tender to his family our sincere condolence in this their great bereavement.   W. H. H. MILLER,
                    SAMUEL O. PICKENS,
                    NOBLE C. BUTLER,
                    LEWIS C. WALKER,
                    EDGAR A. BROWN.

Filed Sept. 26, 1895.

Silas D. Coffey

1839-1904

- Born February 23, 1839, in Owen County, Indiana.

- Entered Indiana University in 1860, but withdrew when the Civil War erupted.

- Carried a copy of *Blackstone's Commentaries* with him during his military service.

- Studied law and opened an office in Bowling Green, Clay County, Indiana, after returning from the war.

- Was an active participant in the Republican Party.

- Named to the Thirteenth Circuit Court bench in 1881.

- Elected to the Indiana Supreme Court in 1888, serving from January 7, 1889, until January 7, 1895.

- Died March 6, 1904, in Brazil, Clay County, Indiana.

MAY TERM, 1904—VOL. 162.   697

Memorial of Silas D. Coffey.

MEMORIAL OF SILAS D. COFFEY,

EX-JUDGE OF THE SUPREME COURT.

May it Please the Court:—On behalf of the members of the bar of Clay
county, I present to the court the following memorial adopted by that
bar on the 7th day of March, 1904, in commemoration of the life and
character of the Honorable Silas D. Coffey, an ex-judge of this court.

Judge Coffey was born in Owen county, Indiana, on the 23rd day of
February, 1839.   After a brief illness he departed this life at Manatee,
Florida, at 8 o'clock p. m., on Sunday, March 6, 1904, aged sixty-five
years and twelve days.

He was reared on a farm, and attended the common schools until, in the
year 1860, he entered the State University at Bloomington.   When the
War of the Rebellion broke out he enlisted in the three months' service,
and when the call for three years' troops was made he enlisted for that
period in the Fourteenth Indiana Regiment, and remained with it until
June, 1863, when, owing to ill-health, he was transferred to the Veteran
Reserve Corps, and later was honorably discharged from the service.
While in the army he carried a copy of Blackstone in his knapsack, and
studied it in camp and whenever opportunity offered.   He began the practice of law in Clay county in 1864, and continued in the practice until,
in the year 1881, he was appointed judge of the Thirteenth Judicial Circuit
of Indiana, to fill the vacancy occasioned by the death of the Honorable
Solon Turman.   At the ensuing election in 1882, he was elected judge of
that circuit for the full term of six years.   As a trial judge his rulings
and decisions were always fair and impartial, ever striving to see that
justice was done to litigants.   In appeals to this court, his decisions were
generally affirmed.

In 1888 he was elected judge of this court and served the full term of
six years.   While on the supreme bench many grave constitutional questions came before the court.   Among them the statute of 1891, redistrict-
ing the State, was declared to be unconstitutional in an able opinion
written by him.   The statute providing for the "Australian System" of
voting was assailed, and in an exhaustive opinion written by him it was
held valid.   The fee and salary law of 1891 was also upheld in an able
opinion written by him, and many other important decisions were rendered in which he participated while on the bench of this court.

As a member of this court his opinions bore evidence of that care and
thought in their preparation which are characteristic of the upright,
conscientious judge.

After his term of service on the supreme bench expired, he resumed
the practice of law in Clay county and continued alone in the practice
until in the year 1900, when he formed a co-partnership with Ex-Judge
Samuel M. McGregor, which continued to the time of his death.

698   SUPREME COURT OF INDIANA,

Memorial of Silas D. Coffey.

With the exception of his service on the circuit and supreme bench, he practiced his profession in Clay and surrounding counties for a period of forty years, with a success rarely attained by any other member of the bar.

He won for himself a high reputation as a successful and skilful practitioner. His advice and assistance were often sought by the younger members of the bar, and were always freely given. To them he was ever kind and magnanimous, and none will miss him more than they.

In his dealings with his fellow men, he was frank, candid and absolutely honest, never seeking or taking an undue advantage. In his social relations he was most genial and affable, kind-hearted and benevolent.

He was a devoted husband and an indulgent and affectionate father. His home was filled with the sunshine of happiness.

He has gone from our midst forever, from this life to the life eternal. Let us cherish the hope, so dear to our hearts, that in a brighter and happier world than this we shall meet and know our loved ones and friends again.

None in this world can escape the ordeal through which he has passed. Of death it has been tersely said :

"There's nothing can escape thee here,
    What e're that object be,
Things that all powerful appear,
    Are subject still to thee."

And so it is, and ever will be to the end of time.

In conclusion, I move that the memorial herewith presented be ordered spread upon the records of this court as an enduring testimonial of the life and worth of our deceased brother.

[Presented by Hon. Geo. A. Knight.]

RESPONSE BY THE CHIEF JUSTICE.

Silas D. Coffey was entrusted by the people of this State with one of the most responsible, although not the most glittering of its tasks. To the discharge of that trust he brought a large measure of capacity and great faithfulness. He bore an honorable and a conspicuous part in the history of this court. It is entirely fitting that the sketch and appreciation of his life which you have presented should be spread of record among the proceedings of this court, and published in the forthcoming volume of its reports. It is so ordered.

Allen Zollars

1839-1909

- Born September 3, 1839, in Licking County, Ohio.

- Graduated from Denison University (Granville, Ohio) in or about 1863 with a bachelor's degree.

- Studied law briefly in Ohio before entering the University of Michigan Law School.

- Received a law degree from the University of Michigan in 1866.

- Served as the Fort Wayne city attorney from 1869 to 1875.

- Appointed the first judge of the Allen Superior Court in 1877.

- Served in the House of Representatives of the Indiana General Assembly in 1869.

- Served in the Indiana Supreme Court from January 1, 1883, to January 7, 1889.

- Died December 20, 1909, in Fort Wayne, Allen County, Indiana.

In Memoriam.

May it Please the Court:

As a member of the bar of this court, I respectfully suggest to the court the death, on December 19, 1909, at his home in Fort Wayne, Indiana, of the Hon. Allen Zollars, a judge of this court from January 1, 1883, to January 7, 1889, and that on December 22, 1909, at a meeting of the Allen County Bar Association, held in the city of Fort Wayne, the following memorial, commemorative of the deceased, was adopted, and I was directed to present the same to this court, with the request that it be entered in the records of this court and published in a volume of its decisions.

The members of the Allen County Bar Association, and their associates from elsewhere in the State, assembled upon the occasion of the death of their brother, Judge Allen Zollars, desire to pay this tribute to his life and memory.

At this moment we think of him first as lawyer and judge. It is given to few men to spend so many years in the profession, and to fewer still to spend them so successfully and in such devoted and unremitting toil. The law was to him a mistress with no rival in his affections. He delighted in it. No astronomer, geologist or naturalist ever loved his science more than Judge Zollars loved the law. Literature and poetry were no more attractive to him than the dry volumes of legal text-books and reports. His professional career was an ideal one. Coming to Fort Wayne with little acquaintance, and no business connections or influences to help him, he began practice with the petty cases and small pay which come to a strange young lawyer. But his industry and thorough work soon attracted attention. Every case he tried was an advertisement, and, until he took his seat on the Supreme Bench, his course was one of continual advancement.

(xl)

James McCabe

∽ 1834-1911 ∽

- Born July 4, 1844, in Darke County, Ohio.

- Moved to Kosciusko County, Indiana, and then to Illinois as a child.

- Began formal education at seventeen years of age while working as a section hand for the Monon Railroad in Crawfordsville, Montgomery County, Indiana.

- Decided to practice law after attending a trial in Crawfordsville.

- Studied law in his spare time while teaching school in the winter.

- Admitted to the Indiana bar in 1871.

- Was an avid Democrat and twice ran unsuccessfully for the United States Congress.

- Elected to the Indiana Supreme Court in 1892, serving one six-year term from January 2, 1893, until January 2, 1899.

- Died March 23, 1911, in Williamsport, Wayne County, Indiana.

In Memoriam.

JAMES McCABE.

James McCabe was born in Darke County, Ohio, on July 4, 1834. As a young man, for a time, he was a teacher. In 1861, he commenced the practice of law at Williamsport, Indiana, and, for the remainder of his life was a resident of Warren County. In 1892, he was elected a judge of this court, and, as such, served the term of six years.

Judge McCabe's professional career extended over the period of half a century, and embraced the time of Indiana's progress from a pioneer condition to a place of foremost rank among the States of the Union; and this half century of Indiana's remarkable advancement was due, in the main, to the intelligence, integrity and industry of a great group of citizens, of this State, of which he was a typical and conspicuous member.

Like many others of his time, he was not a graduate of any law school, but, in his profession, was self educated and self trained; yet, from this school of experience, he emerged as one of the State's leading advocates, and his loyalty to clients, his zeal in their behalf, and his untiring industry in the preparation of their causes justly earned for him a reputation as a capable lawyer, and one that was by no means confined to the locality where he practiced his chosen profession. He was a logician, and possessed a remarkable power to state clearly and concisely any proposition he sought to present, and this power was well recognized by the bench and bar of Indiana.

His opinions, delivered while a member of this court, speak for themselves. They cover a time when many novel and important questions were presented and determined. They are marked by the industry and discriminating logic which characterized his career, and, it is but fair to say, greatly enriched the jurisprudence of this State.

(xxxix)

There was another than a professional side of Judge Mc-Cabe's life that is not unworthy of mention here. His kindly, loyal spirit attracted friendships that were life enduring. A conspicuous evidence of this characteristic was noted in the memorial exercises held by the Warren County Bar Association, at Williamsport, on Sunday, May 7, 1911.

Wm. J. Bryan, journeyed from Nebraska to attend that meeting, and, in eloquent phrase, recounted the virtues and achievements of his departed friend.

Judge McCabe lived to enjoy the highest honors at the disposal of his chosen profession, to see his adopted State among the foremost in progress and achievement; he lived to see his two sons achieve honorable eminence in his own life profession, and, in the fulness of time, he rested from his labors. His career is worthy the emulation of Indiana's youth.

James Henry Jordan
1834-1911

- Born December 21, 1842, in Woodstock, Virginia.

- Served with the 45th Indiana Volunteers, 3rd Indiana Cavalry, participating in all of the important battles involving the Army of the Potomac during the Civil War.

- Attended Wabash College (Crawfordsville, Indiana), but graduated from Indiana University in 1868.

- Read law with Judge William A. Porter and Thomas C. Slaughter.

- Admitted to the Indiana bar in 1868.

- Received a law degree from Indiana University in 1871.

- Served as the prosecuting attorney of the Common Pleas District, which included Morgan, Johnson, Monroe, Brown, and Shelby Counties.

- Served as the city attorney of Martinsville, Morgan County, Indiana, from 1873 to 1885.

- Elected to the Indiana Supreme Court in 1894, serving three terms from January 7, 1895, until his death.

- Died April 5, 1912, in Martinsville, Morgan County, Indiana.

JAMES HENRY JORDAN.

James Henry Jordan, late a Justice of this court, was born in Woodstock, Shenandoah County, Virginia, December 21, 1842, and came to Harrison County, Indiana, with his father in 1853, settling near Corydon. His mother died in 1849.

His education began in the common schools of Harrison County. At the age of eighteen years he enlisted in the Indiana Legion, and in July, 1861, joined the First Indiana Cavalry, later known as the Forty-fifth Regiment, under command of Conrad Baker, later Governor of Indiana.

Judge Jordan participated in seventy-six pitched battles, engagements and skirmishes, and was with Sheridan on the raid against Richmond, Virginia, in May, 1864, and with General Wilson on his raid against Richmond which resulted in the destruction of the Weldon Railroad, one of the chief bases of supplies of the Confederate Army at and about Richmond. He was in the fierce struggles at South Mountain, Antietam, Gettysburg, Brandy Station, Chancel-

(xl)

lorsville and the Wilderness. He was wounded at Gettysburg, and again at Culpepper Court House, November 8,
1863, from which latter wound he was a sufferer for the remainder of his life, but with the courage peculiar to him,
no complaint is known by his friends to have ever escaped
him: he bore it with a soldier's fortitude.

At the close of the civil strife he attended Wabash College two terms, and was graduated from Indiana University
in 1868, and in 1871 was graduated from the Law Department of that institution. He began the practice of law at
Clinton, Missouri, where he resided one year, and then came
to Martinsville, Indiana, where he resided until his death.
He was engaged in active practice of the law until he became a member of this bench in January, 1895, and of which
he was a member at the time of his death. He held many
positions of minor importance, and discharged their duties
with marked fidelity and ability. He occupied this bench
continuously more than seventeen years, during a period of
great industrial and economic activity, and when many
questions of grave importance were before the court. He
had a capacity for broad views upon all subjects, and an
analytical mind, which impressed themselves upon the jurisprudence of the State. He had rare courage, a keen sense
of public duty, an unwavering confidence in the institutions
of the country, a loyal fealty to his friends, and a broad
charity.

We direct that this memorial to him, who, in war and in
peace, gave signal evidence of a high standard of citizenship, professional honor, intrepid courage, and marked integrity, be spread upon the records of the court.

Byron Koscuisko Elliott

1835-1913

- Born September 4, 1835, in Butler County, Ohio.

- Attended public schools and Hamilton Academy (Ohio) until 1849.

- Came to Indianapolis, Marion County, Indiana, in 1850 with his father.

- Attended the Marion County (Indiana) Seminary, studied law, and admitted to the bar in February 1858.

- Elected city attorney of Indianapolis in May 1859.

- Served as a captain in the 132nd Indiana Volunteers, rising to the rank of an adjutant-general during the Civil War.

- Served as city attorney for Indianapolis from 1865 to 1869.

- Elected judge of the Marion County criminal court in 1870.

- Re-elected to the city attorney post (Indianapolis) in 1872.

Continued

Byron Koscuisko Elliott

 continued

- Elected to the Superior Court of Marion County in 1876.

- Elected to the Indiana Supreme Court in 1880, serving from January 3, 1881, until January 2, 1893.

- First president of the Indiana Law School of Indianapolis.

- Practiced law with his son, William F. Elliott, after his service on the bench.

- Died November 19, 1913, in Indianapolis, Marion County, Indiana.

BYRON K. ELLIOTT.

Byron K. Elliott was born near Hamilton, Ohio. At the age of fifteen he came to Indianapolis with his father, General William J. Elliott. Indianapolis was his home from that time until his death at the age of nearly seventy-eight years.

His education in the school was completed at Indianapolis in the Old Seminary in University Park. When twenty-two years old he was admitted to the bar, and the next year was elected to the important office of City Attorney for the City of Indianapolis.

He saw service in the civil war as a Captain of Infantry, and on the staff of General Milroy. He resumed the practice of law and was again elected City Attorney. In 1870 he was, without opposition, elected Judge of the Criminal Court of Marion County. He resigned the position of Judge and became City Solicitor, and afterward was again City Attorney. In 1876 he was elected Judge of the Superior Court of Marion County, and in 1880 quitted that office to become Judge of the Supreme Court of Indiana, where he served twelve years.

All the official positions held in civil life by Judge Elliott were such as required the labor of a lawyer. He lectured to law classes in different colleges, and was one of the founders of the Indiana Law School and its first President. Collaborating with his son, he was an author of a number of text-books. Of these, "The Work of the Advocate," "Appellate Procedure", "Roads and Streets", "General Practice", "Evidence" and "Railroads" are the most highly valued. In addition to all this he delivered many public addresses and often contributed to legal publications.

For almost half a century he devoted himself to the study and practice of the law, to teaching it to young men, to collecting it in books, and to declaring it with the authority of a Judge. It has rarely been given to any man to cover

(xlii)

so completely the whole field of activity peculiarly appropriate to a lawyer. So frail of body that his adult life
was almost one long illness, the enormous amount of valuable work accomplished recalls such heroic lives as those of
Alexander Pope and Francis Parkman.

His mind was singularly alert and his memory of precedents remarkable. He worked with almost incredible
rapidity. Abundance of ideas and exuberance of diction
called for restraint and control. For this purpose he
read Aristotle and other great exemplars of brief and
severe expression. To his intellectual equipment was added
absolute purity of character. His ideals were high and his
life has been and will long continue to be an inspiration to
all coming within its influence, and especially to young men.

Judge Elliott was one of the gentlest and kindliest of men.
His judgments of his fellow men were intelligent and discriminating, but were always charitable and expressed without harshness or malice. As a judge his patience and respectful attention never failed or faltered. He was always
polite, courteous and considerate of the rights and feelings
of others. To oblige he would concede everything but his
manly independence of action and convictions of justice
and duty. These he yielded to no man under any circumstances. Always and everywhere he so bore himself toward judges, associates, opponents and all who came in
contact with him, that we may well say of him as Tenny-
son said of his lost friend:

> "And thus he bore without abuse
> The grand old name of gentleman
> Defamed by every charlatan
> And soiled with all ignoble use."

With such a career it need hardly be here declared that
he was an able and most industrious lawyer. In sixty volumes of the decisions of the Supreme Court of Indiana lies
the permanent record of his exposition of the law as applied
to a great variety of important subjects. No words of ours
can add to or affect that magnificent memorial.

While he valued the favor and esteem of his fellow citizens, his services as a public officer were always such that indebtedness if any was to, rather than from him. Happy the state that should have no servants but such as he!

Byron K. Elliott bid adieu to earth attended by all that should accompany old age, "honor, love, and troops of friends". The influence of his life will, in itself, be a very real and most splendid immortality.

> JOHN B. ELAM.
> WM. H. H. MILLER.
> JOHN S. DUNCAN.
> ALEXANDER C. AYERS.
> LEWIS C. WALKER.
> QUINCY A. MYERS.
> CALEB S. DENNY.
> DANIEL W. HOWE.

Ordered spread of record.

> SPENCER, C. J.

John Vestal Hadley
1840-1915

- Born sometime between 1839 and 1842 in Hendricks County, Indiana.

- Attended Northwestern Christian University (now known as Butler University) for one year.

- Enlisted in the Union Army in which he served three and one half years before the end of the Civil War.

- Wounded twice during the war.

- Managed to escape from a prisoner of war camp in Columbia, South Carolina, and walk to Tennessee, where he found a camp of Union troops.

- Wrote *Seven Months a Prisoner,* an account of his experiences as a prisoner during the Civil War.

- Studied at the Indianapolis Law School.

- Admitted to the bar in 1866.

- Served as a circuit judge for eleven years.

- Served on the Indiana Supreme Court from January 2, 1899, to January 2, 1911.

- Died November 17, 1915, in Danville, Hendricks County, Indiana.

In Memoriam

JOHN VESTAL HADLEY

Remorseless Time that knows not the weight of years has passed and, stopping not like other conquerers to note the ruin it has wrought, has called from among the living in the full fruitage of an eventful life another that has graced the bench of this Court and added luster to the shining lights that preceded him.   John Vestal Hadley is dead.

He was born October 31, 1840, in Hendricks County, Indiana, and died amid the scenes of his nativity, November 17, 1915.   How long, and yet how short was the span of that life!   He crowded into that brief space more of the joys and sorrows of life than are allotted to the ordinary individual. Born on a farm amid the toil and hardships of pioneer life, he, by his own zeal and endeavors arose above the surroundings and secured in his youth the rudiments of an education, which, added to in his more mature years, placed him among the front ranks of the foremost thinkers and workers in his chosen profession.   He served three and one-half years as a soldier in defense of his country; twelve years as Judge of the Hendricks Circuit Court; one term as State Senator from his native county; and from January, 1899, to January, 1911, was Judge of this court.   In all positions to which he was chosen he knew no motive but justice and no guide but his conscience.   His aims and ambitions were of the highest order.   He exercised and practiced the spirit

(xxxi)

xxxii   IN MEMORIAM

of law rather than the letter, and to his mastery of
the principles of his profession he added the spirit
of justice and equity, which were the ruling passions
of his life.   From his wonderful storehouse of learning and wisdom manifested in all his actions as
lawyer and judge, the present and future have
received a rich heritage.   In his declaration of legal
principles, he was clear, but faultlessly concise, not
wasting in repetition the beauty of the doctrine
declared.   His opinions were exhaustive without
being verbose and will ever remain "a pillar of cloud
by day and a pillar of fire by night" to men of his
profession who may follow in his luminous footsteps.
Adding to his legal qualifications, he manifested a
beauty of soul and symmetry of thought that
endeared him to all men of every class and
character with whom he came in contact.

His life is a beautiful example, worthy the emulation of all men, especially the lawyer.   His aim
was to do justice and yet to temper that justice
with mercy.   We could not wish, no man could desire, a better epitaph than that which is universally
written or, at least, thought by all his friends and
acquaintances, "He loved his fellow man."   It may
be said of him as of the Shepherd King of old, "He
served his day and generation well, and fell asleep."
He touched every chord in the harp of life.   His
past is secure; his future is with Him who said,
"Well done thou good and faithful servant, enter
thou into the joys prepared for you from the foundation of the world."

This memorial to John Vestal Hadley, presented
by Erwin, J., was unanimously adopted and ordered
spread of record.   LAIRY, C. J.

Timothy Edward Howard
〜 1837-1916 〜

- Born January 27, 1837, in Northfield, Michigan.

- Attended the University of Michigan from 1855 to 1857, but received his degree from the University of Notre Dame in Indiana.

- Left college in 1862 before graduation to enlist in the 12ᵗʰ Michigan Infantry during the Civil War.

- Wounded at Shiloh, Tennessee, during the Civil War and then discharged because of a disability.

- Admitted to the Indiana bar in 1883.

- Held a variety of public offices, including Inspector of Schools (1858), South Bend city councilman (between 1878 and 1913), St. Joseph county clerk (1879-1883), Indiana state senator (1887-1891) and South Bend city attorney (1888-1891).

- Served on the Indiana Supreme Court from January 2, 1893, to January 2, 1899.

- Held the office of president of the Indiana Fee and Salary Commission and a member of the Commission for Revising and Codifying the Laws of Indiana.

- Died July 9, 1916, in South Bend, St. Joseph County, Indiana.

In Memoriam

TIMOTHY E. HOWARD.

Timothy Edward Howard, *nomen, clarum et venerabile,* was born upon a farm in Northfield township, Washtenaw county, Michigan, January 27, 1837; he died at South Bend, July 9, 1916, in the eightieth year of his age.   After a country-school course of instruction he attended the union school at Ypsilanti, Michigan, and there was under the instruction of one of the greatest educators of Michigan, Joseph Estabrook.   At the age of eighteen he entered the University of Michigan. The next few years of his time were divided between attending the university, managing the home farm, and teaching country school.   In 1859 he became a resident of St. Joseph county as a student of Notre Dame University, which he attended for about three years.   Before coming to South Bend he was elected, at the age of twenty-one, to his first public office, viz., school inspector of his native township.

February 5, 1862, as a volunteer, he enlisted as a private in the Twelfth Michigan Infantry. In the battle at Shiloh two months later he was so severely wounded that he was discharged from the service. He returned to St. Joseph county in the summer of 1862 and was immediately employed as professor of English literature at Notre Dame University and so continued for many years.

In 1878 he was elected a member of the common council of South Bend and served for six years. He again was elected councilman and served during the years 1910 to 1913, inclusive. He was city attorney

(xxxii)

TIMOTHY E. HOWARD.

during the years 1888 to 1891, inclusive. He also served as county attorney of St. Joseph county. In 1878 he was elected clerk of the St. Joseph Circuit Court and served four years in that position. In 1886 he was elected a member of the Indiana State Senate and in 1890 was re-elected for a second term; but, in 1892, before the expiration of his second term, he was elected a judge of the Supreme Court of Indiana and served for a term of six years. His term began on January 2, 1893, and four days after, on January 6, he filed his first opinion in the case of *Harlan* v. *Logansport Natural Gas Co.*, 133 Ind. 323. His last opinion is a memorandum filed November 29, 1898—*Husted* v. *National Home Building and Loan Association*, 152 Ind. 698. His last formal opinion was filed October 25, 1898—*Copeland* v. *Town of Sheridan*, 152 Ind. 107—and involved the validity of an ordinance of the town of Sheridan. His last published opinion was filed November 16, 1898—*Chicago and Eastern Illinois R. Co.* v. *State*, 153 Ind. 134—which involved the validity of a statute of the State regarding the consolidation of railroads. Because of a petition for a rehearing the case was held up for nearly a year and was not passed on until long after Judge Howard retired from the bench, but his opinion was upheld. If time permitted it would be interesting to refer in detail to some of the important cases which came before our Supreme Court during Judge Howard's term and in the decision of which he participated, but we refer to only one class of cases—those involving riparian rights. In each case of this class coming before the Supreme Court during his term he wrote the opinion. The twenty volumes of Indiana reports are enriched and adorned by the logical reasoning and the clear, lucid English of the many opinions which he wrote.

Of many men history only records, "He held public

TIMOTHY E. HOWARD.

office," and then is silent. This was not true of Judge Howard. He held many public positions—positions of public trust—but in these he accomplished lasting and beneficial results; and as a part of this memorial, we shall recite the following, *in perpetuam rei memoriam.* When a member of the State Senate he was the author of the bill providing for the removal of the limestone ledge in the Kankakee river at Momence, as a result of which the drainage of the Kankakee river in Indiana was greatly improved. He assisted in framing the Australian ballot law in 1889, the first ballot reform in Indiana. He introduced in the Senate in 1891 the bill for the establishment of the Appellate Court, and was the author of the bill for the Indiana tax law of 1891.

After his retirement from the Supreme bench he was appointed by a Governor who differed from him in politics as a member of the State Fee and Salary Commission, and became the president thereof; and, at the tax conference held at the Pan-American Exposition in Buffalo in the same year, he was chosen by the same Governor—Durbin—to explain the Indiana tax law. From 1903 to 1905 he served as one of the members of the commission appointed by Governor Durbin for the codification of the statutes of the State. This commission reported bills which were enacted into laws regarding the criminal code and procedure, cities and towns, which for the first time gave this State a systematic organization and classification of cities and towns and legislation regarding the same; also, regarding drainage and highways.

As a lawyer Judge Howard belonged rather to the class of counsellor than of advocate. He was a solicitor, rather than a barrister. He settled controversies and disputes, rather than litigated them. If we had the English system of classification of lawyers, he would

TIMOTHY E. HOWARD.

have stood as a fine example of that highest class known to the profession—the old family solicitor.

He was a charter member of the State Bar Association of Indiana, his name being second on the list of the signers of the articles thereof. He served almost constantly upon its important committees, had been its vice-president, and frequently prepared and read before the association papers of great interest and value. At the time of his death he was preparing for the annual meeting of the association a paper upon the subject, "The Authority of the Ordinance of 1787," but on the day on which he was to have read it before the association he was borne to his last resting place.

In the Psalms it is written, and also in the ritual of the dead: "The days of our age are three score years and ten; and though men be so strong that they come to four score years, yet is their strength then but labour and sorrow; so soon passeth it away, and we are gone." Was this true of Judge Howard? By reason of strength he came to the four score years, all of which were filled with useful service to mankind. Many positions of public honor and trust he filled; the result was not to his private emolument and profit, but was a wise and substantial service to the public good. He held and administered private trusts, never to the loss or even the inconvenience of the beneficiaries.

Judge Howard was fortunate in that he lived to see and feel and know the respect, the honor and the affection in which he was held by his fellow-citizens. He enjoyed in his latter years some of the rewards of his useful and well-spent life, for he must have known, as he met and greeted his fellow townsmen, the high regard in which he was held by them and which was shown and exhibited by their attitude and manner toward him.

It may be said of him, in the language of the book of

TIMOTHY E. HOWARD.

Ecclesiastes: "A good name is better than precious ointment, and the day of death than the day of one's birth."

To him, death, life's last visitor, has come. He knocked at the door; it was opened. He bowed to no one, greeted no one, but to his host he said, "Come," and the two passed out together across that threshold over which there is no return.

And so we leave him, and say, as did the Romans of old to their dead: "Farewell, forever, we shall all follow thee in whatsoever order nature may permit."

Richard Kenney Erwin
⟶ 1860-1917 ⟵

- Born July 11, 1860, in Union Township, Adams County, Indiana.

- Educated in the district school and attended one term at Methodist College (Fort Wayne, Indiana).

- Taught school in Allen and Adams counties while studying law.

- Admitted to the Indiana bar in 1886.

- Elected to the Indiana House of Representatives in 1891 and re-elected in 1893.

- Served as county attorney of Adams County, Indiana, from 1889 to 1897.

- Became judge of the Twenty-sixth Indiana Judicial Circuit from 1901 to 1907.

- Elected to the Indiana Supreme Court in 1912 by a margin of 120,330 votes, receiving the most votes ever given to any Indiana Supreme Court Justice.

- Served on the Indiana Supreme Court from January 6, 1913, until his death.

- Died October 5, 1917, in Fort Wayne, Allen County, Indiana.

RICHARD K. ERWIN.

Richard Kenney Erwin was born on a farm in Union township, Adams county, Indiana, on July 11, 1860, a son of David and Mary Ellen (Need) Erwin, his father being one of the early pioneers who settled in that section of the State in 1839.   The son was one of Indiana's products of the log-house home and the country school.   Both of his parents departed this life before he arrived at majority and on the death of his father the young lad had cast upon him the charge of the home farm and the care of the family.   He finished the common schools of his home district and then completed a course at the Methodist College in Fort Wayne. He taught school for one year in Allen county and for six years in his native county of Adams, during which period he took up legal studies in the office of France and Merriman of Decatur, Indiana.   After his admission to the bar in 1886 he went into the general practice and with his acquired knowledge of the law and his natural abilities soon developed into a good lawyer. His progress was ever onward, marked and steady.   He was elected by the people and served as representative to the Indiana General Assembly for the sessions of 1891

(xxxvi)

RICHARD K. ERWIN.

and 1893, being one of the legislative leaders of that period. His record in that capacity was enviable. From 1891 to 1896 he served as county attorney for Adams county and in 1900 was elected judge of the twenty-sixth judicial circuit, serving with distinction and credit from 1901 to 1907. He was the Democratic nominee for judge of the Supreme Court of the State in 1906, but was defeated at the polls by Hon. Leander J. Monks. In 1907 he opened law offices in Fort Wayne and went into the general practice, where he at once took rank with the leading members of the bar in that part of Indiana. As an advocate he was retained in and successfully tried a number of cases in the courts of northern Indiana and in the courts of last resort, commanding state-wide attention. In 1912 he was again a candidate for judge of the Supreme Court and was again opposed by Judge Monks. Judge Erwin was elected by the largest vote ever given to a candidate on the state ticket, defeating his opponent by 120,330 votes. On January 7, 1913, he qualified as judge under the commission issued to him as a result of that election and served as a member of the court until his death on October 5, 1917.

Judge Erwin was married at Monroeville, Indiana, on January 17, 1883, to Miss Luella A. Wass who, with their five children, survives him. The children are: Dr. Harry G. Erwin, Huntertown, Indiana; Mrs. Robert Allison, Indianapolis; Richard W. Erwin, law librarian, Indianapolis; David Erwin, a student at Purdue University, and Miss Francile Erwin, who lives with her mother in the Erwin homestead at Fort Wayne. Judge Erwin was an active Scottish rite, thirty-second-degree Mason, a member of the Elks, and the Knights of Pythias.

His career and service as a member of the Supreme Court of his State, like all service rendered by him, was

RICHARD K. ERWIN.

notable and honorable. At the time of his death he was the presiding Chief Justice of the court. His opinions —and there are many of them on subjects of great moment—are concise and clear, his reasoning sound and his diction perfect. Personally, although resolute in conviction, he was mild in manner and his character was lovable. His mind ever turned to philosophy and to the literary classics, and from the masters of the latter he was always ready with a quotation to illumine the occasion. He was not what in this day is termed a "case lawyer," but his viewpoint was that of the fundamentals. He saw the merits of the controversy with an eye which applied the never failing test in appellate judicial procedure,—Has substantial justice been done? Such manner of judge was he that he was much loved by those who knew him and much admired and respected by those who knew of him.

His mind was atune with the poets and often his own thoughts would be by him rhythmically recorded. The closing stanza of a poem of his own composition, entitled "God's Plan," will best illustrate his idea of the world beyond and of the immortality of the soul—

"And all the tears we here have shed
    Within this vale of sorrow's night,
May, over There, when we are dead,
    Be sparkling gems, in God's clear light.

It is ordered that this memorial be entered of record and printed in the official reports and a copy mailed to the family of the deceased.

SPENCER, C. J.

July 30, 1918.

Reprinted from Jacob P. Dunn. *Indiana and Indianans*, Vol. 3
(Chicago: The American Historical Society, 1919), facing p. 1501

William Henry Harrison Miller

1840-1917

- Born September 6, 1840, in Augusta, New York.

- Taught school at the age of fifteen.

- Resumed studies and graduated from Hamilton College (Clinton, New York) in 1861.

- Moved to Maumee City, Ohio.

- Enlisted as a private in the 84th Regiment, Ohio Volunteer Infantry in 1862.

- Discharged from the Army as a lieutenant three months later in September 1862.

- Studied law in Toledo, Ohio, with Morrison R. Waite, who would later become chief justice of the Supreme Court of the United States.

Continued

William Henry Harrison Miller

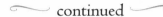 continued

- Worked as superintendent of schools in Peru, Miami County, Indiana, while continuing his study of law.

- Admitted to the Indiana bar in 1865.

- Moved to Fort Wayne, Allen County, Indiana, to form a law partnership in 1866.

- Joined the Indianapolis firm of Porter, Harrison & Hines (of which the future twenty-third president of the United States, Benjamin Harrison, was a member) in 1874.

- Appointed United States Attorney-General by President Benjamin Harrison in 1889, serving until 1893.

- Returned to private practice of law in Indianapolis, Marion County, Indiana.

- Served as a trustee at Hamilton College (New York) from 1893 to 1898.

- Died May 25, 1917, in Indianapolis, Marion County, Indiana.

WILLIAM HENRY HARRISON MILLER.

William Henry Harrison Miller was born in Oneida county, New York, on September 6, 1840. He was graduated at Hamilton College in 1861 where he afterward received the honorary degree of Doctor of Laws. He served as a lieutenant in 1862 in the Eighty-fourth Ohio volunteers in the War of the Rebellion. After a very brief apprenticeship in the office of Morrison R. Waite, later Chief-Justice of the United States, he was admitted to the Bar at Peru, Indiana, in 1865, removing the next year to Fort Wayne. There he practiced his profession until 1874 when he removed to Indianapolis to enter the firm of Harrison, Hines and Miller. From 1889 to 1893, he was Attorney-General of the United States, under his former partner, President Benjamin Harrison. At the end of his term at Washington, he returned to continue the practice at Indianapolis until he retired a few years ago. For many years during President Harrison's activity in politics, Mr. Miller was one of the legal advisors of the Republican Party upon political and constitutional questions. He was a charter member of the Indianapolis Bar Association and was its president in 1884 and 1885. He was trustee of Hamilton College for many years and an elder in the First Presbyterian Church at Indianapolis. He was a member of the Indianapolis Literary Club. The office of Attorney-General is the only political office he ever held.

Benjamin Harrison, on two occasions, called W. H. H. Miller to a higher place and each time his act was justified by events, for the young law partner measured up to the requirements of the junior membership in one of the leading firms of the State just as later the Attorney-

(xxxix)

WILLIAM HENRY HARRISON MILLER.

General, inexperienced in official life, measured up to the high rank of his ablest predecessors in the office. That he thus made good in performance and character was due of course to his natural endowment and his professional discipline. He had a robust, active and comprehensive mind, an intellectual zest for knowledge, and an unstudied and matter-of-fact way of using his powers. His training was the captivating give-and-take of the courtroom and the conference chamber when in matters of large moment he met able judges, strong rivals and far-seeing counsellors. For a man of his mind and temperament, it was an ideal environment, which roused every faculty to its highest effort and checked every limitation to its smallest handicap, and which made him an all-round lawyer rather than a specialist.   Indeed it would not have been congenial to him to have been a specialist; he had too pronounced a curiosity in the metaphysical sense to have been content with a single groove or an isolated department. Moreover, his mind was not much given to the process of detailed refining after the manner of the analytical type but, on the contrary, it worked along lines of relation and co-ordination.   His reasoning had the force of breadth and cumulation rather than of precision and keenness.   His method was Vulcanlike; "And upon the anvil stand he set the mighty anvil; and he forged the links that could be neither broken nor loosed, so that they should stay firm in their place."

It is evident from the foregoing facts, that as lawyer Mr. Miller was self-taught. With the qualification of a vigorous and active mind, he had the added qualifications of industry, independence and self-confidence. It fell to his lot to be so circumstanced in the kind of business which came to him that all of his strong characteristics were brought into full play, and it was only in keeping with his character and temperament that he

WILLIAM HENRY HARRISON MILLER.

never sought to restrain any of his native forces. He might truthfully have said of himself, what the Master of the Rolls, Sir George Jessel, is reported to have confessed in this language: "I may be wrong, but I never have any doubts." This does not mean that he was so self-centered as never to forget a case that he had lost and to persist in criticizing the court which had not agreed with him. On the contrary, he was always open-minded, and whatever the final issue might be, he accepted it as a conclusion. This quality of open-mindedness was the keystone of the arch of his professional career. He was not a radical who wished to wipe out old land-marks and to set up new standards, but he was progressive and he was firmly convinced that with the normal changes of society legal principles must also advance and expand. He was a born student and accordingly familiar with the precedents, but he always developed them into principles and he followed the spirit and trend of the cases rather than their literal content. He disliked dicta and half-truth; and for this reason, he had a wholesome disrespect for legal maxims as maxims, saying that they were almost always misleading because either they stated a proposition too broadly or they stated it too narrowly and taken all in all they were only epigrammatic statements that were not susceptible of expansion to meet concrete facts. He was a partisan in the sense that he was always loyal to his clients' interest and he would not, for the sake of personal consistency or to avoid the lessening of his own prestige by a defeat, decline to take and contend for a position that was not backed by an authority or an analogy. The fortunes of business and his intellectual tendencies brought it about that he became a pioneer in cases of novel impression. One has only to look through the court reports of his time to see that he was a lawyer who dared to blaze the way and many cases il-

WILLIAM HENRY HARRISON MILLER.

lustrate how successfully he did blaze the way in the development and expansion of the law in principle and procedure. From his individual point of view he never acted upon the dictum of playing safe. In the interests of his client he forgot himself and his own professional reputation. He was not less bold in action than he was bold in thought and he never made a compromise with his honest convictions lest he might be charged with being either a tyro in the practice or an iconoclast in the law. This means that he was intellectually courageous and professionally progressive and it was these very characteristics that made him a man of prominence in the American Bar. He was aggressive but not contentious; he was firm in his convictions but not obstinate; he was masterful but not dictatorial. And it stood him in good stead to be aggressive, positive and masterful because he was resourceful intuitively and by his learning; but it was the resourcefulness of strength and knowledge and not the resourcefulness of adroitness and subtlety. He might change his position, but he always struck from the shoulder and he disdained to make use of a cryptic thrust.

The best-remembered case in which Mr. Miller was concerned while he was United States Attorney-General was one remarkable for its spectacular and dramatic features—*In re Neagle,* 135 U. S. 1. It is a fine example of Mr. Miller's clearness of vision when a new principle arises and of his willingness to bear the brunt of making that principle vital and permanent. During the absence of President Harrison from Washington, word came to the Department of Justice at Washington that David S. Terry and his wife were threatening personal violence to Justice Stephen J. Field in retaliation for his recent decision against them and that it would be unsafe for Justice Field to hold court in California. Mr. Miller conceived the theory that it was the duty of

WILLIAM HENRY HARRISON MILLER.

the Department of Justice to give Justice Field whatever personal protection was possible, and he instructed the United States Marshal to provide a special bodyguard for this purpose. The expected assault took place. Neagle, as the deputy marshal specially charged with the protection of the Justice, killed Terry. He was charged with murder in the California court and released by Justice Sawyer of the United States Circuit Court on habeas corpus. The case was appealed to the Supreme Court of the United States and affirmed.

The question was novel. The department of Justice was now called upon for the first time to take affirmative action, and determine upon a course of violence, if need be, to protect the person of a judge and in this way enforce the authority of his court. When President Harrison returned to Washington, the Attorney-General had already acted and had so acted that the President feared he had exceeded his constitutional powers. Mr. Miller's duty under the law was clear enough to him and in his luminous way he proceeded to convert the President to his own way of thinking. When the case reached the Supreme Court of the United States, Mr. Miller argued it in person. The result was a decision sustaining the course of the Attorney-General from the beginning and strengthening the authority of the National Government. Like the case of *In re Debs* which followed it, and accepted its authority, that of *In re Neagle* became a leading case in support of the governmental doctrine that the nation may exert whatever power it needs to uphold its authority, and that the law which confers that power is the supreme law of the land. Its doctrine was extended in *Logan* v. *United States*, 144 U. S. 263, to protect persons under arrest for federal offense against state interference and mob violence.

United States v. *Texas*, 143 U. S. 621, involving the

WILLIAM HENRY HARRISON MILLER.

right of a nation to sue a state to determine the state's boundary as against the adjoining federal territory, is another illustration of Mr. Miller's readiness to assume the burden of presenting a case of novel impression when it was easily possible for him to have assigned the work to one of his assistants in the office, but he recognized the importance of the issue and faced it as he conceived it his duty to do, because the question was new and large rights of the National Government were concerned.

All through his life, whatever his hand found to do, he did with all his might and in the open day. He did this not because he was impelled by personal ambition, but because of his fidelity to duty whether the duty was an obligation to his client or the higher obligation to his country. He never sought to evade responsibility in whatever way responsibility came. Above all other obligations he placed the obligations of citizenship as paramount and demanding the highest fealty. He maintained that fealty by keeping abreast of the times and with resolute courage and admirable poise doing and saying the things that in his honest judgment would best promote the welfare of his city, his state and his country. He never tried to carry water on both shoulders and he always called a spade a spade, so that at times it took not a little from his ease of mind that he was so uncompromisingly outspoken in criticism of men and measures that at the moment had the advantage of popular favor. Yet even if it became evident later that his views were erroneous no one could successfully maintain that he was insincere, selfish or unpatriotic. Nature made him a plain, blunt man. But nevertheless he studied to inform himself. He was a reader in the domain of politics, economics and literature. He strove to know the best of the thought of the world. Such reading, of necessity, made his mind more

WILLIAM HENRY HARRISON MILLER.

catholic and less partisan. His judgments were the result of deliberation and even if they were not always right, they were certainly righteous, and they were not the prejudiced opinions of one who lags superfluous on the stage and can only hark back to the authority of a forgotten leader, but were the conclusions of a modern whose premises were facts of today. In this sense of keeping abreast of the times, Mr. Miller did not grow old, and it was just because he thus continued youthful that his patriotism was vital and constantly fresh and his attitude of mind toward the law was the attitude of the progressive lawyer who is a prophet of change that is remedial and tonic.

Entrusted with five talents, this man, now quietly and without reluctance entering into the presence of the Master, returns to Him ten talents.

W. A. KETCHAM.
EDWARD DANIELS.
C. C. SHIRLEY.
CHARLES A. DRYER.
CHARLES W. MOORES.

May 28, 1917.

Once more the Indiana State Bar Association meets to pay tribute to the memory of one of its charter members; who, ripe in years and in honor, has passed the grim frontier of death.

William Henry Harrison Miller, farmer's son, student, teacher, soldier, lawyer, statesman, and friend, was born in Oneida county, New York, September 6, 1840, and died in Indianapolis, Indiana, May 25, 1917. Although born in the state of New York, for more than two-thirds of his life he was a citizen of Indiana, so that we can well claim him as our own. His education —begun in that typical American institution, the common school, followed by a term in Whitestown Semi-

WILLIAM HENRY HARRISON MILLER.

nary and by graduation from Hamilton College—was continued to the day of his death in the great university of observation and experience and by association in the field of literature with the best and brightest minds of all time.   His study of the law was begun in the office of Morrison R. Waite, Chief Justice of the Supreme Court of the United States, while that eminent jurist was practicing law at Toledo, Ohio, but those who knew Mr. Miller best know that he never ceased to be a student.   He was admitted to the bar at Peru, Indiana, in 1865, where he remained for a short time.   In 1866 he removed to Fort Wayne, and became a partner of William H. Combs, later one of the judges of the Supreme Court of the State of Indiana.   Subsequently Robert B. Bell was admitted to the firm of Combs, Miller and Bell. In 1874 he removed to Indianapolis, to become a partner in the firm of Harrison, Hines and Miller.   Indianapolis has since been his home.

During the incumbency of Benjamin Harrison as President, he served as Attorney-General of the United States.   Since that time, he has been associated at various times as partner in the practice of the law at Indianapolis, with Ferdinand Winter, John B. Elam, Cassius M. Shirley, his son Samuel D. Miller, William H. Thompson, and Frank C. Dailey.   During his career as a lawyer, he was associated with and from time to time pitted against many of the ablest lawyers our country has produced, and was recognized as their peer. Among his cotemporaries at the Bar of Indiana were such men as Benjamin Harrison, Thomas A. Hendricks, Joseph E. McDonald, John M. Butler, Abraham Hendricks, Conrad Baker, John H. Baker, Joseph A. S. Mitchell, Byron K. Elliott, James L. Worden, John Morris, James L. Fraser, James I. Best, John T. Dye, and Addison C. Harris, all of whom recognized in him a worthy and formidable adversary.   Benjamin Harrison, who was

(xlvi)

WILLIAM HENRY HARRISON MILLER

not only a great lawyer, but a shrewd and keen judge of the legal ability of others, paid him a high tribute when he appointed him Attorney-General. No man was in better position to know and appreciate his fitness for that place than the man who had for years been his partner in the practice of the law. The ability displayed by him in solving the many grave and difficult problems that arose during his four years incumbency in that position fully vindicated the judgment of Mr. Harrison. He had a thorough knowledge of the fundamental principles underlying our system of government, and withal he had the courage of his convictions. This was forcibly illustrated by his prompt action in the Terry case.

David S. Terry had been Chief Justice of the Supreme Court of California. His successor was Stephen J. Field. Terry was known as a violent and reckless man. Angered by some things said in debate by United States Senator David C. Broderick, he challenged him to fight a duel and killed him. Terry's influence in California was such that he escaped merited punishment. Judge Field was appointed by President Lincoln a judge of the United States Supreme Court. As one of the judges of that court, he was to preside at a term of court in California, while Mr. Miller was Attorney-General. Judge Terry declared that Judge Field should not preside at that term of court, and threatened that he would kill him if he attempted to do so. Mr. Miller at once took the position that an independent and fearless judiciary was essential to the maintenance of our form of government, and that it was the duty of the Executive Department to furnish the judges ample protection. He accordingly instructed the United States Marshal to use any means necessary to protect Judge Field from the threatened danger. Terry attempted to carry his threat into effect, and was killed by a deputy United States

WILLIAM HENRY HARRISON MILLER.

marshal. The marshal was indicted for murder, and through the influence of Terry's friends would doubtless have been convicted and punished, if Mr. Miller had not intervened and secured a judgment by the Supreme Court of the United States vindicating his action. Mr. Miller acted without precedent, but by his action secured the establishment of a principle of incalculable value.

While occupying the position of Attorney-General, he also established another precedent, which it is to be regretted has not always been followed by his successors. He personally and carefully investigated the character and qualifications of every applicant for appointment to judicial office, and no man received a judicial appointment during the entire administration of Benjamin Harrison who could not show an unblemished record as a lawyer and as a man.

This occasion does not require a revision of Mr. Miller's work, but in him were combined the tireless worker, the conscientious and well-informed lawyer, the clear and logical reasoner, and the cogent and forceful speaker. He had a vivid sense of humor, and was master of a keen and cutting sarcasm that, while it could penetrate the armor of sophistry and self-sufficiency, left no venom in the wounds it inflicted. His reading was extensive and varied, and his fund of general information made him a most interesting conversationalist. He was warm hearted and sympathetic, and his friendships were strong and lasting.

At this crisis in our country's history, it would not be just to Mr. Miller's memory to omit reference to his sturdy and patriotic Americanism. While he was of English and Scotch ancestry, his father was a native of New York and his mother was a native of Massachusetts. His love of his native country was without bounds, and he gave unhesitating and unstinted support

WILLIAM HENRY HARRISON MILLER.

to every measure necessary to the maintenance of our national honor.

ROBERT W. MCBRIDE,
ERNEST R. KEITH,
THOMAS E. DAVIDSON,
WILLITTS A. BASTIAN,
JOHN L. RUPE,
JAMES WASON,
Committee.

Adopted at a joint meeting of the Indianapolis Bar Association and the State Bar Association of Indiana held May 28, 1917.

ELMER E. STEVENSON,
President of Indianapolis Bar Association.

Attest:

JOSEPH J. DANIELS,
Secretary of Indianapolis Bar Association.

This memorial is adopted and ordered spread of record in the order book of this court.

R. K. ERWIN, C. J.

June 29, 1917.

Leander John Monks

⟶ 1843-1919 ⟵

- Born July 10, 1843, in Winchester, Randolph County, Indiana.

- Studied at Indiana University from 1861 until 1863.

- Admitted to the Indiana bar in 1865.

- Practiced with various attorneys until 1878, when elected as a circuit judge.

- Elected to the Indiana Supreme Court in 1894 and served from January 7, 1895, until January 7, 1913.

- Served as chief justice of the Indiana Supreme Court in 1904.

- Practiced law in Indiana.

- Wrote *Courts and Lawyers of Indiana* (1916), an extremely valuable book about the legal system and lawyers in Indiana from 1816 to 1916.

- Died April 19, 1919, in Indianapolis, Marion County, Indiana.

In Memoriam

LEANDER J. MONKS

Leander J. Monks was born in Winchester, Indiana, July 10, 1843, and died in Indianapolis, April 19, 1919. He was the son of George W. and Mary A. Monks. His father came to Randolph county, Indiana, from Ohio a few years after the organization of the State of Indiana. He was a pioneer in Indiana, a prominent and useful citizen, and did his full part in developing and building up the county. Judge Monks made Winchester his home throughout his entire life, although during the later years he spent the greater part of the time in Indianapolis, where his official, professional and business relations required his presence. The foundation of his splendid educational accomplishments was laid in the public schools of Indiana and by an attendance of three years at Indiana University. Judge Monks belonged to a family of Methodists and throughout his life affiliated with, and took an active interest in, the work and purposes of the Methodist Episcopal Church. On August 3, 1865, he and Lizzie W. White were married. To this union were born four children. His home life was ideal in every way.

Judge Monks was a member of the Sigma Chi college fraternity and of the Columbia and Marion clubs of Indianapolis. He was a member, also, of the Independent Order of Odd Fellows and of the Masonic fraternity, attaining in the latter order the thirty-second degree rank. Throughout his life Judge Monks was a wide reader of the best in history, economics, poetry and fiction. He was a man of broad and real culture and

(xxviii)

LEANDER J. MONKS.

possessed an extensive and valuable fund of general information. His private library of general literature was one of the best in Indiana. Prior to his judicial career he took an active interest in each successive political campaign in every capacity, except as a public speaker, being chairman of the Randolph County Republican Committee and also a member of the State Central Committee and the State Executive Committee of his party.

Judge Monks commenced the practice of law at Winchester in 1865. He soon took a prominent place in his profession and was recognized as a capable, industrious and skilful lawyer. In 1878 he was elected Judge of the Twenty-fifth Judicial Circuit, then composed of Randolph and Delaware counties. He was re-elected to that position in 1884 and 1890, at the latter date the circuit consisting of Randolph county alone. He was elected a judge of the Supreme Court of Indiana in 1894 and re-elected in 1900 and 1906. He was renominated in 1912, but at the election he was defeated with his party. Prior to his election to the circuit bench he practiced law successively with Colonel M. B. Miller and Hon. E. L. Watson, both now deceased, and with Judge W. A. Thompson, now judge of the Delaware Circuit Court. Soon after retiring from the Supreme Bench he opened a law office in Indianapolis in partnership with John F. Robbins, Harry Starr and James P. Goodrich, now Governor of Indiana. Later the firm was dissolved and Judge Monks continued the practice of law in Indianapolis without any partnership relation until his death.

Judge Monks, although a prominent public man in Indiana for many years, was not a public speaker. As a counselor in guiding and directing those who were trial lawyers in the discharge of their duties as such, he was a master. As a consequence great trial lawyers

LEANDER J. MONKS.

sought his counsel and guidance in the courtroom. By
the public Judge Monks was best known and will be
longest remembered for what he did in his judicial
capacity. We think of him first as a lawyer and judge.
Rarely does it come to a lawyer to spend as many years
on the bench as did Judge Monks.

With such a career it need hardly be here declared
that he was an able and most industrious lawyer. In
forty-one volumes of the decisions of the Supreme Court
of Indiana lies the permanent record of his exposition
of the law as applied to a great variety of important
subjects. No word of ours can add to or affect that
magnificent memorial. As a member of the highest
court in his state his reputation as a judge is much
broader than his state. His work placed him in the
front ranks of the foremost thinkers and workers in
his chosen profession. His mind was singularly alert
and his memory of precedents remarkable. He worked
with almost incredible rapidity both as a trial and appellate judge. His opinions written while a member
of the Supreme Court bear evidence of an exhaustive
examination of the authorities and indicate the great
talents and profound knowledge that he possessed. His
opinions were clear and concise and contained the most
lucid statements of the law. They were exhaustive
without being verbose and will ever remain "a pillar of
cloud by day and pillar of fire by night" to men of his
profession who may follow in his luminous footsteps.
Lawyers and judges both within and without the state
turn to his opinions with a feeling of confidence that
thereby they will be safely guided to a just solution of
any legal problem confronting them. As a judge he
was so well versed in the fundamental principles of the
law that he was naturally a conservative. He believed
in the Constitution and in the fundamental and long-
established principles of the law. He believed in or-

LEANDER J. MONKS.

derly development—in leading down slowly from precedent to precedent. He kept constantly before his mind the principle that stability and orderly development and progress in a state are the things most to be desired. He believed that the law should be so declared and adhered to by the courts that every person could safely rely thereon in his personal conduct and business transactions. He realized fully that men in all relations of life should be able safely to act on the law as declared by the courts of appellate jurisdiction in carrying out their various transactions. He believed that the doctrines announced by the courts of appeal should not be departed from except in the presence of a necessity growing out of a substantial error in a former opinion. He recognized very vividly that a material change in the law throws into confusion business and other matters entered into on the faith of former decisions. He therefore believed that the widest possible scope should be given to the principle of *stare decisis*. He liked the law. It was his master. He delighted in it. Always was he ready to discuss legal principles and their application. No scientist ever loved his science more than Judge Monks loved the law.

Happy the state that has no servants but such as he. The influence of his work as a lawyer and judge and the example of his life as a private and public citizen will in themselves be a very real and most splendid immortality. It may be said of him as of the Shepherd King of old, "He served his day and generation well, and fell asleep."

The above memorial presented by George H. Batchelor, secretary of Indiana State Bar Association, is accepted and ordered filed and spread on the records of the Supreme Court.

March 19, 1920.   TOWNSEND, C. J.

John Henry Gillett

⟨ 1860-1920 ⟩

- Born September 18, 1860, in Medina, New York.

- Educated in the public schools of Valparaiso, Porter County, Indiana.

- Studied law under the direction of his father, Judge Hiram A. Gillett, and was admitted to the Indiana bar in 1881.

- Practiced law from 1881 to 1885.

- Taught law at Northern Indiana Normal School (now Valparaiso University, Valparaiso, Indiana).

- Appointed city attorney of Valparaiso, Indiana, in 1885.

- Served as Deputy Attorney General of Indiana from 1886 until 1890.

Continued

John Henry Gillett

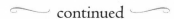 continued

- Moved to Hammond, Lake County, Indiana, in 1890 and formed a law partnership with Peter Crumpacker, which continued until June 1892.

- Appointed judge of the Thirty-first Indiana Circuit Court and then elected for a full term at the next election (1892-1902).

- Appointed to the Indiana Supreme Court in 1902, filling the vacancy created by the resignation of Judge Baker.

- Elected to the Indiana Supreme Court for a full term in November 1902 and served until January 3, 1909.

- Authored two legal volumes: *Criminal Law* and *Indirect and Collateral Evidence.*

- Died March 16, 1920, in Hammond, Lake County, Indiana.

━━━━━━━━━━

JOHN H. GILLETT

With sadness and solemnity, we are called upon as lawyers to record the passing to the Unseen of our beloved friend and neighbor, John H. Gillett. No practitioner in this part of the state has attained a higher standing as a lawyer, a jurist, a citizen, a husband and friend than he.

Born in New York State on September 18, 1860, and coming to Indiana when a mere boy, Judge Gillett combined the traditions and experiences of the East with the rugged and vigorous life of the Middle West. The son of an eminent lawyer and jurist, he was constantly in the atmosphere of his chosen profession, and his admission to the bar at the age of twenty-one was but a natural and easy step. After six years in general practice, including service as city attorney of the city of Valparaiso, he became Deputy Attorney-General of Indiana, in 1887, in which capacity he served for four years with great credit to himself and his state. He found time, notwithstanding the arduous duties of his service in this office, to prepare the text of his widely used work on Criminal Law. He came to Hammond in 1891, at the close of his second term as Deputy Attorney-General, to engage in the general practice of law. On July 2, 1892, he was appointed circuit judge, and served in that capacity with the highest degree of acceptability until January 25, 1902, when he was chosen by the Governor of Indiana, to become a member of the Supreme Court. This appointment was approvingly acclaimed throughout the state as a recognition of the exceptional merit and qualifications of the

(xxxii)

JOHN H. GILLETT.

appointee. At the next general election he was elected for a full term of six years, and his opinions rendered during that time are considered by all lawyers as evidencing a profound knowledge of the law, and classic as to diction, showing a clear conception of the controversy, stated in such clear and unambiguous terms that the layman could read and understand. After his retirement from the bench, he returned to Hammond, and resumed the practice of his chosen profession, taking at once a foremost place at the bar, and continued in active practice up to a very short time before his death.

Of his capacity as a lawyer and thinker, not only judges and lawyers, but all who knew him, alike bear witness. Never given to frivolity, but always, even though serious, possessed of a sunny disposition, he surrounded himself with lasting friendships. At the beginning if his chosen life's work, he was imbued with the idea of proficiency, and by close application and industry seldom equaled, and very rarely excelled, he had developed a mentality which analyzed the most intricate legal problems, leaving them clear and understandable. He was not only a great man intellectually, but morally and spiritually, though always humble and unostentatious. His home life and thoughtful devotion to his life companion were singularly inspiring.

To borrow the language he used within recent months in paying tribute to one of his life-long friends and professional associates, "His leave-taking caused poignant regret, particularly to those associated with him in professional life." It is with a sense of real loss in the passing of John H. Gillett that the undersigned submit this tribute to his memory, as the report of the committee of the Lake County Bar Association, that the same may be spread of record by the secretary of this association, and that a copy thereof be spread on the

JOHN H. GILLETT.

order books of the courts of Lake county, and filed with the Supreme Court of Indiana; that a copy be sent to his son and sister.

V. S. REITER,
L. L. BOMBERGER,
D. E. BOONE,
Committee.

This memorial accepted and ordered spread of record.

March 30, 1920.   TOWNSEND, C. J.

Lawson Moreau Harvey

1856-1920

- Born December 5, 1856, in Plainfield, St. Joseph County, Indiana.

- Educated in the public schools of Indianapolis, Marion County, Indiana and attended the Indianapolis Classical School.

- Studied at Butler College (Indianapolis, Indiana) and at Haverford College in Haverford, Pennsylvania.

- Graduated from the Central Law School in Indianapolis in 1882.

- Entered the private practice of law.

- Elected to the Marion County Superior Court in 1894.

- Returned to private practice in 1898.

- Returned to the Marion County Superior Court in 1907.

- Served on the Indiana Supreme Court from January 1, 1917, until his death.

- Died June 25, 1920, in Indianapolis, Marion County, Indiana.

In Memoriam

LAWSON M. HARVEY.

LAWSON M. HARVEY was born in Plainfield, Indiana, December 5, 1856, and died at his home in Indianapolis, June 25, 1920.   He was of Quaker stock, the son of the late Thomas B. Harvey, one of Indiana's greatest physicians, and came to Indianapolis when a boy eight years old.   He was educated in the public schools, the Indianapolis Classical School, Butler College, Haverford College at Philadelphia, and the Central Law School of Indianapolis, from which he graduated in 1882, and at once began his life profession in the general practice of law, devoting his efforts almost solely to the civil practice.   His high character and conscientious efforts soon brought him a clientage among some of the best business people of Indianapolis.   In 1884 Alexander C. Ayers was elected to the circuit bench in Marion county, thus dissolving the law firm of Ayers and Brown. Edgar A. Brown, later judge of the circuit court, and Mr. Harvey thereupon formed the firm of Brown and Harvey.   After three years of service Judge Ayers quit the bench and returned to the general practice with the firm, Ayers, Brown and Harvey. In 1890 Mr. Brown was elected to the circuit bench and after that Mr. Harvey practiced alone until 1894, when he was elected Judge of the Marion Superior Court.   At the end of the term he refused renomination and formed a law partnership with William A. Pickens, Linton A. Cox and Sylvan W. Kahn as Harvey, Pickens, Cox and Kahn. He remained in the practice with this firm until 1907, when he was

(xxxii)

LAWSON M. HARVEY.

appointed by Governor Hanly to the newly created position of Judge of the Superior Court of Marion County, Room 4. He held this position until 1908, when he returned to the general practice with his son, Horace Harvey, under the firm name of Harvey and Harvey, continuing this practice until 1917, when he took his seat on the bench of the Supreme Court of Indiana. The remaining three and one-half years of his life were devoted to the conscientious service of the state, and he was stricken while at his post of duty. The story of his work on the Supreme bench is told more completely in the published reports of the state than can well be done in this memorial. He approached every question with an open mind and weighed all argument in just scales before forming any opinion on the controversy.

During his years of private work he was the legal counsel and attorney for some of the best men and institutions in Indianapolis.

His life work was not confined solely to the field of the law. He was one of the directors of the Bertha Ballard Home Association, The Home for Friendless Colored Children, an active worker in his church and in politics, and affiliated with the Chamber of Commerce, the Marion Club, and the Columbia Club. He was for several years the Secretary of the Indianapolis Bar Association and an active participant in its work at all times, serving as president of that association during the year 1907.

The public esteem in which Judge Harvey was held grew with every day of his life. In his professional career he had the full confidence of his clientage and the respect and kindly feeling of his adversaries. Probably the strongest single impression made by him on the bench, the bar, and the public, was that he was under all circumstances and at all times a perfect gentleman. He was active as a practitioner for about twenty-eight

LAWSON M. HARVEY.

years, more active in the courts than the average lawyer, and as judge for about ten years. During these years he was almost always dealing with controversies in which brethren of the bar of high standing and ability were contending. It can truthfully be said that he lived almost forty years in an atmosphere of contention and as a participant in strife, without once doing or saying, or even thinking, anything bordering on the ungentlemanly or discourteous, and no judge, lawyer, or layman, whether associate or adversary, will gainsay this statement, but all observers will confirm it. His gentlemanly qualities and even temperament gave him in high degree the judicial character. This equipoise, partly inborn, but strengthened, cultivated and maintained by conscientous labor in what he believed to be the greatest of all sciences, was the predominating element in his character, and the quality that made him a just judge and safe counsellor.

Many of us assume that in all legal controversies, the human element, being ever present, must sometimes cause the course of justice to go awry. Judge Harvey never took this view. He was always confident that a lawyer should be able to decide with precision how any controversy must finally end and should be able to bring about justice if his case were properly prepared. This confidence which he felt in the law as a science was so implicit and his belief that right would prevail so serene, that a defeat in the *nisi prius* court never created any doubt in his mind as to the ultimate end of the controversy. The fact that there might be an adverse decision in the court of last resort which must be distinguished or overruled did not deter him if by this study he thought that decision unsound.

About six months ago he lost by death the wife with whom he had lived in loving congeniality for nearly forty years. He never recovered from the shock of this

(xxxiv)

LAWSON M. HARVEY.

loss and his family and friends are comforted by the thought that they are now reunited.

Judge Harvey was cut off in his prime when his state had much use for him—stricken at his desk while engaged in his work, and after three days of quiet under the cloud of a darkened mind, passed peacefully away. He was always ready for the end, conformably to the philosophy of Marcus Aurelius, which has come down to us bright through the rubbish of two thousand years.

> "Pass then through this little space of time conformably to nature and end thy journey in content, just as an olive falls off when it is ripe, blessing nature that produced it, and thanking the tree on which it grew."

Moses B. Lairy,
W. A. Ketcham,
Edgar A. Brown,
William A. Pickens,
Ralph Kane,
Committee.

The above memorial reported at a joint meeting of the State Bar Association of Indiana, held in the court room of the Supreme Court of Indiana, in the city of Indianapolis, Indiana, on June 28, 1920, was adopted and ordered spread of record by the Supreme Court of Indiana.

Townsend, C. J.

Edwin Pollock Hammond
◠ 1835-1920 ◡

- Born November 26, 1835, in Brookville, Franklin County, Indiana.
- Moved to Columbus, Bartholomew County, Indiana, at the age of fourteen.
- Studied law in Indianapolis, Marion County, Indiana.
- Admitted to the senior law class at Asbury—now DePauw—University (Greencastle, Indiana) in 1857.
- Admitted to the Indiana bar in 1858.
- Practiced law for two years prior to enlisting in the Union Army during the Civil War.
- Appointed as a circuit judge after the War, and won the election to a full term in 1878.
- Served on the Indiana Supreme Court from May 14, 1883, until January 6, 1885.
- Returned to private practice briefly in 1885, and then served two more years as a circuit judge.
- Served as a trustee of Purdue University.
- Died January 27, 1920, in Lafayette, Tippecanoe County, Indiana.

𝕴𝖓 𝕸𝖊𝖒𝖔𝖗𝖎𝖆𝖒

EDWIN POLLOK HAMMOND, LL. D.

BE IT REMEMBERED, That upon June 28, 1921, at a session of the Supreme Court of the State of Indiana, at Indianapolis, present:

> Mr. Chief Justice Townsend,
> Mr. Justice Myers,
> Mr. Justice Willoughby,
> Mr. Justice Ewbank,
> Mr. Justice Travis,

the following proceedings were had:

HON. MOSES B. LAIRY: May it please the Court, The Tippecanoe County Bar Association at a recent meeting appointed a committee, consisting of Hon. Henry H. Vinton, Judge of the Tippecanoe Superior Court, Hon. Charles R. Milford, Joseph A. Andrew, Dan W. Simms and myself, to present to this Court a picture of the late Edwin Pollok Hammond, who from May 4, 1883, to January 1, 1885, was an honorable and honored member of this bench, and to prepare a statement in the nature of a Memorial and present the same to this Court.

Judge Hammond was born at Brookville, Indiana, on the 26th day of November, 1835. He studied law with his brother, Abraham Hammond, afterward Governor Hammond. Later he graduated from the Law Department of Asbury University with the degree of B. L. The following year he entered upon the practice of his profession at Rensselaer, and was thus engaged at the beginning of the Civil War, at which time he enlisted, entering military service as Captain of Company A in the 87th Ind. Vol. Inf. He served throughout the en-

(xxxvi)

EDWIN POLLOK HAMMOND.

tire war. On March 22, 1862, he was promoted to Major of his regiment, and in November following was made Lieutenant-Colonel of the same regiment. He participated in many of the most sanguinary struggles of the Rebellion and at one time was wounded in battle.

Upon his discharge from the army he returned to Rensselaer and again resumed the practice of his profession. In 1873 he was appointed by Governor Thomas A. Hendricks Judge of the 30th Judicial Circuit, was subsequently elected to the same position and re-elected in 1878.

On May 14, 1883, he was appointed by Governor Albert G. Porter, Justice of this Court to fill the vacancy occasioned by the appointment of Mr. Justice Woods to the Federal bench.

At the close of his service upon this bench, January 1, 1885, he again resumed the practice of his profession at Rensselaer, but in November, 1890, was once more called to preside as Judge of the 30th Judicial Circuit. This service continued until 1892, when he resigned and moved to Lafayette to become a member of the firm of Stuart Brothers and Hammond. This copartnership continued until the death of Charles B. Stuart, when the firm became Stuart, Hammond and Simms, which continued uninterruptedly for a period of seventeen years, when the title of the firm was changed to Stuart, Hammond and Stuart, which continued until January 1, 1919, when it again became Stuart, Hammond and Simms, and thus continued to the date of his death on January 27, 1920. The degree of LL.D. was conferred upon Judge Hammond by Wabash College in 1892.

For many years it was my great pleasure and good fortune to know Judge Hammond, both as a lawyer and a judge, intimately and well. He challenged and ever held my highest respect—my supreme confidence. His life and character were such that multitudes of friends,

EDWIN POLLOK HAMMOND.

in every section of the state, were endeared to him. Most happy shall I be if when called upon to close my career I can find, as he did, an abiding place in the love and confidence of my fellowmen.

I present Dan W. Simms, a member of the committee and for many years prior to and at the time of his death a partner and intimate friend of Judge Hammond, who will present the Judge's picture to the Court and offer a brief tribute to his memory.

DAN W. SIMMS: May it please the Court, on behalf of the Tippecanoe County Bar Association, the family of Judge Hammond and a host of friends from every walk of life, I present to this great tribunal—the Supreme Court of Indiana—this excellent likeness—this picture of the Judge, furnished by the family.

I present it hoping that the Court may find it convenient and desirable to place it in this court room among the pictures of his associates upon the bench, each of whom, I believe, preceded him to the Great Unknown.

It seems to us especially fitting that these brief exercises should be held in this forum.   Upon this bench was much of his constructive work done, and at this bar for a period of more than a quarter of a century he appeared perhaps more frequently than any other member. Among the records of this Court there will be found in enduring form exhaustive briefs prepared by him upon many of the most important, interesting and intricate phases of the law.   In his practice here, as at *nisi prius,* he had but few equals and no superiors.   You all knew him, and to know him was to love him.   As I voice these words you have doubtless been thinking of him as you saw him in life here or elsewhere, on the bench or in the forum, battling for his clients' rights; thinking of him as you saw him at home, or mingling with his fellowmen, or engaging in his party's councils, or as you

EDWIN POLLOK HAMMOND.

had learned of him on weary march or fierce battlefields. Thus shall we all think of and remember him as we saw him in life and in full possession of all of his splendid faculties. But this Judge Hammond of whom we speak and think—this soldier, citizen, lawyer, jurist, scholar—whom for a generation we have so reverently respected, so intimately known and so ardently loved—grew weary just the other day, lay down and, folding tired hands, dozed off into that sleep which we call death—a sleep from which his exhausted mental and physical organisms shall awake no more.

While the shock was yet upon us we carried tenderly the mortal remains—the tenement in which for almost a century his spirit dwelt—to the quiet cemetery yonder overlooking the Iroquois, where rest the ashes of his loved ones gone before, and sadly said good-bye.

We mourn his absence but we dare not complain, for who in all our range of knowledge or acquaintance has been more entitled or better prepared to matriculate and enter upon the curriculum in God's greater University than he.

Poignant, of course, must be the grief of those who linger here, and difficult the readjustment for those who stood in close relationship; but upon us all there rests the great duty to see that his precepts be not forgotten nor his examples disregarded. He was indeed a great—a noble man. The purity of his life, the grasp of his intellect and the breadth of his vision, the kindliness of his heart and the stability of his character—these were the integral factors that an All Wise Providence employed to make of him the wonderful man he was.

Out of absolute integrity of mind and heart his keen, unerring sense of the law, of equity, of justice, took its rise. Out of love of family, home and fellowman there sprang that patriotic impulse which led him on to victory in his nation's cause. Out of environment, in part

EDWIN POLLOK HAMMOND.

created by himself, grew the splendid character, crystal-
lized the ennobling sentiment, and came the potent poise
that marked him as a leader among his fellows.

Judge Hammond's life and achievements are now history. His contribution to that great current fund of
common knowledge which bears the race forward and
upward upon its bosom was tremendous in its volume
and far-reaching in its effect.

He donned, for a longtime wore, and doffed the judicial ermine with never a stain, but with satisfaction to
the bar, credit to himself and great honor to the bench.

His love for his profession was equaled only by the
jealous and zealous care with which he guarded the vir-
tue and the honor of that high calling. The practice
of the law was to him a noble vocation. Never did he
forget that as a lawyer he was a sworn officer of the
court whose duties called for the highest qualities of
mind and heart in assisting the court to arrive at correct conclusions and to dispense evenhanded justice.

His life and his career on the bench and at the bar
demonstrate the theorem "An honest man is the noblest
work of God." No man can achieve even moderate success at the bar or upon the bench who is not inherently
and instinctively honest in thought and deed.

Our duties with relation to Judge Hammond end not
with these memorial exercises—indeed they just begin.
Upon us now rests the responsibility to maintain and
preserve inviolate the high ideals for which he stood.
We must not—we dare not permit ourselves or others
to deviate from the highest standard of legal ethics.
The greatest tribute we can pay to his memory will be
to follow in his footsteps in discharging our relations
to our clients, to the courts, to the body politic, and to
and among ourselves.

The choice is ours to live as he has lived, with the
unshaken confidence of all in the integrity of his inten-

EDWIN POLLOK HAMMOND.

tion, and to die as he died at the very zenith of the love, the esteem and the veneration of a veritable multitude of good and noble men and women who were proud to know and call him friend; or to live the lives of cynics, distrusting and distrusted, while added years but show the narrowing mind, the shriveling, piteous soul, and die at length leaving never a comrade to say "He acted well his part. He did his share and the world is better because of him."

For some of us the journey is almost done; for others just commenced; but whether young or old, I am sure our choice has been pondered well and made—and to each of us I know the life and character of him to whom we do homage here today will stand out as a beacon light and grow brighter and stronger and more inspiring as the seasons come and go and the years multiply. And to you, Judge Hammond, whom we all love and venerate; you! whose earthly form has been given back to earth from whence it came, but whose spirit lingers here and communes with us, in the names of the lawyers and judges of the state you loved so much I pledge our devotion to the high ideals that animated you. Our motives shall be pure. Our lives shall be clean and upright. Our work shall be unremitting to maintain the highest standard of legal ethics to the end that justice shall prevail and your memory shall eternally abide.

TOWNSEND, C. J.: It was not my privilege to know Judge Hammond personally and intimately; but, when I was a boy, ambitious to become a lawyer, he was an inspiration to me. When he came before the court in the county where I resided, I adjourned everything and attended the trial. He had the ease and grace of a master in his profession. He was adroit, pleasing, persuasive, powerful. It is too bad that so much of the method of such a man is lost to the profession, when he is gone from sight and hearing.

Quincy Alden Myers

∼ 1853-1921 ∽

- Born September 1, 1853, near Logansport, Cass County, Indiana.
- Received his bachelor's degree from Dartmouth College (Hanover, New Hampshire) in 1875.
- Studied law with the city attorney of Logansport for over a year.
- Attended the Union (now Albany) Law School in New York, receiving a law degree in 1877.
- Admitted to the Cass County bar in 1877 and worked in several law partnerships in Logansport.
- Served as the Logansport City Attorney, from 1885 to 1887, and the Cass County Attorney, from 1903 to 1909.
- Elected to the Indiana Supreme Court and served from January 4, 1909, to January 4, 1915.
- Failed to win the Republican nomination for governor of Indiana in 1916.
- Returned to private law practice in Indianapolis, Marion County, Indiana.
- Died December 27, 1921, in Indianapolis, Marion County, Indiana.

In Memoriam

QUINCY ALDEN MYERS.

QUINCY ALDEN MYERS was born on a farm near Logansport, Indiana, September 1, 1853, the son of Isaac N. and Rosanna Justice Myers. His father was a pioneer farmer in Indiana. Mr. Myers received his elementary education in the country schools and in the Logansport Presbyterian Academy. He later became a student in Northwestern Christian College in Indianapolis, the University of Michigan and Dartmouth College; and was graduated from the latter institution with the degree of bachelor of arts in 1875. He was graduated with the degree of bachelor of laws from the Albany Law School, then krown as Union College, at Albany, New York, in 1877; and also received the degree of master of arts from Dartmouth College in 1880. On the completion of his course in the law school he was admitted to the practice of law in Cass county and in the Supreme Court of this state.

From August 14, 1877, until 1882 he practiced law in Logansport with Maurice Winfield. In 1882 he formed a partnership with John C. Nelson for the practice of law. This partnership continued until 1909, when Mr. Myers became by election a member of the Supreme Court of Indiana. He and other Republicans were elected in the state election in 1908, notwithstanding the fact that a Democratic Governor and Lieutenant-Governor were elected. He served as a judge of the Supreme Court until 1913. Soon after the completion of his term he associated himself with Edward E. Gates in the practice of law in Indianapolis. Samuel M. Ralston joined them when his term as Governor ended, and

(xlii)

QUINCY ALDEN MYERS.

the firm has since practiced law under the name of Myers, Gates and Ralston.

Mr. Myers married Jessie D. Cornelius of Indianapolis March 3, 1886. The widow and one daughter, Marlissa J., the wife of Dr. Joel Whitaker, of Indianapolis, survive him. A daughter died a number of years ago. The home life of Mr. Myers was splendid and ideal in every respect.

During his practice of law in Logansport Mr. Myers served as city attorney from 1885 to 1887 and as county attorney of Cass County from 1895 to 1897 and from 1903 to 1909.

He was a life-long and active Republican. In 1900 he was one of the Republican presidential electors and in 1916 he was a candidate for the Republican nomination for Governor against Governor James P. Goodrich and Governor Warren T. McCray.

He was a member of the Columbia, the Marion, the Woodstock and the Century Clubs in Indianapolis. He belonged to the Association of Indiana Pioneers, the State Historical Society and the Indianapolis Bar Association, the Indiana State Bar Association and the American Bar Association. Mr. Myers' activities extended outside of legal and political fields and he was always a participant in civic and sociological movements. He was a member of the board of trustees of Depauw University and an active member of the American Institute of Criminal Law and Criminology, an organization representing the various groups interested in problems connected with the administration of justice, including the treatment of criminals. In character and purpose this organization was without precedent in the history of the United States. It represented the first instance of co-operative effort among those interested in a better system of criminal justice. Mr. Myers was one of the most vigorous promoters of that cause

QUINCY ALDEN MYERS.

and rendered a fine service to it.   He was president of the Institute in 1913 and 1914 and when its annual meeting was held in Indianapolis in 1920 he was chairman of the local committee in charge of arrangements.   He attended and took an active part in the recent meeting at Cincinnati, and was chosen one of the vice-presidents and a member of the executive board.

As a lawyer he was so well versed in the fundamental principles of the law that he was naturally a conservative.   He believed in the constitution of his state and his nation and in the fundamental and long established principles of law.   He believed above all else in orderly and progressive development in matters of law and in principles of government.   He kept constantly before his mind the principle that stability and orderly development and progress in a state are the things most to be desired.   He believed that the law should be so declared and adhered to by the courts that every person could safely rely thereon in his personal conduct and business transactions.

As a lawyer he was known for the remarkable diligence with which he looked after the interests of his clients.   He was a born student and accordingly familiar with precedents, but he always developed them into principles; and he followed the spirit and trend of the cases rather than their literal content.

He was aggressive but not contentious; he was firm in his convictions but not obstinate; he was masterful but not dictatorial.

Not only was he splendidly and deeply learned in the law as a science, but he was thoroughly conversant with the rules of practice of it.

He brought to the service of the state as a supreme judge this thorough equipment, together with a habit of hard work and thoroughness and the highest integrity and a profoundly conscientious desire to administer

QUINCY ALDEN MYERS.

exact justice. His service on the supreme bench was a service of constant and tireless industry that has rarely, if ever, been excelled, as is shown in the reported cases during his term from 1909 to 1915.

His work as a Supreme Court judge was one of marked credit to himself and to his profession. His opinions on questions of public importance won wide and favorable comment. He wrote the opinion of the court in many cases of great importance and far-reaching effect.

The subject covered by his opinions include combinations in restraint of trade, wills, taxation, contracts, laws regulating intoxicating liquor, employers' liability, the writ of mandamus, highways and various other legal questions.

One of his earlier opinions sustained the constitutionality of the law of 1899 directed against combinations in restraint of trade.

In one of his numerous opinions on laws relating to intoxicating liquor, Judge Myers said that a voter could authorize an agent to sign a remonstrance against any and all applications for license to sell liquor, and that the power of attorney continued until revoked by the voter who executed it. At that time it was a live question in Indiana. The liquor interests naturally challenged signatures to one remonstrance after another by agents to whom power of attorney had been given, for this practice enabled the prompt filing of remonstrances without circulating a petition for signatures by the individual remonstrators every time an application for a liquor license came up.

He wrote the opinion in the case appealed from Marion county, testing the constitutionality of the law of 1891, prohibiting a person not a member of a fraternity or lodge from wearing the badge of the order. The law was held constitutional.

QUINCY ALDEN MYERS.

The opinions written by him on questions of taxation are highly regarded by those who administer the tax laws and by others. He set out clearly the doctrine that there may be classification with the limitation, that there must be equalization in the same class.

His opinions bear evidence of an exhaustive examination of the authorities and indicate the great talents and profound knowledge that he possessed. They were comprehensive without *obiter dicta*. They were clear and concise and contained the most lucid statements of the law. Lawyers both within and without the state turn to them with a feeling of confidence that thereby they will be safely guided to a just solution of legal problems confronting them.

Ex-Governor Samuel M. Ralston, a law partner of Mr. Myers, paid the following splendid tribute to him:

"I am very much distressed over the death of Judge Myers. I admired him much before I became associated with him in the practice of law. After I became his partner I grew to love him and I have no hesitancy in saying that he was one of the most beautiful characters I ever knew.

"He was always busy—in fact too busy—and yet I never saw him when he did not have time to consider a question troubling a friend. I never heard him make a discourteous remark to anyone, nor did I ever see him irritated because things did not go his way.

"He was always very earnest in his advocacy of any question or cause he championed, but his earnestness did not cause him to cease to have a gentleman's bearing in his relation with opposing counsel.

"Judge Myers was an excellent lawyer and for many years before he became a member of the Supreme Court of Indiana he enjoyed a large and paying practice. As a Supreme Court judge he prepared his opinions with great care, and I think it will be admitted that they

QUINCY ALDEN MYERS.

rank very high. In his death the state has lost a man who stood not only for law and order, but for a high standard of citizenship, embracing virtues that add to the strength and dignity of the state and nation."

Mr. Myers had a most attractive personality, one that at once attracted men to him. He was most courteous, scholarly and democratic in manner. He always had respect for the finer amenities of life. He was a reader in the domain of law, politics, economics and general literature. He strove to know the best of the thought of the world.

Mr. Myers liked the law and delighted in it. It was his master. Kind but courageous, he lived up to the highest ideals of his profession.

Happy the state that has no servants but such as he.

The influence of his work as a lawyer and judge and the example of his life as a private and public citizen will in themselves be a very real and splendid immortality.

He was the happy warrior, such as every man in arms should wish to be. Entrusted with five talents, in the fullness of time, he returned to his Master with ten talents.

ELMER E. STEVENSON,
JAMES N. NOEL,
W. N. THORNTON,
JAMES A. COLLINS,
JAMES A. ROSS,
Committee.

Memorial

Another has been taken from our circle, leaving a vacant chair which can not be filled, and we are now called upon to record the same in the book of the past.

JUDGE QUINCY ALDEN MYERS, born and reared in Cass County, Indiana, had not yet reached the allotted threescore and ten years when death's summons called him away in body, but not in memory.

His youth, young manhood and middle life was spent with us and the character he sustained during that time was an enviable one, lustrous in its unselfishness, simplicity and rectitude.

As a husband and father, kind, loving and faithful; a friend firm, constant and true; a lawyer, untiring, conscientious and upright; a judge, unbiased, impartial and just; and as a man, plain, honorable and honest.

His life was an example of all the qualities, emblems and virtues that go to make a good man, a worthy citizen, a faithful servant and a just judge.

That this, our expression of love and sorrow for our departed friend and co-laborer, be spread upon the records of our Court and a copy thereof presented to his family, and copies transmitted to the Supreme Court of Indiana, and to the Circuit and Superior Courts of Marion County.

CHARLES E. GARLETT, Chairman,
JOHN C. NELSON,
FRANK W. KISTLER,
GEORGE E. ROSS,
ALBERT G. JENKINS,
Committee on Memorial.

This—Friday—December Thirtieth, A. D., 1921.

This memorial accepted and ordered spread of record January 24, 1922.   EWBANK, C. J.

Reprinted from *Indianapolis Men of Affairs*
(Indianapolis: The American Biographical Society, 1923), p. 642.

Ward Harrison Watson

1859-1932

- Born November 7, 1859, in Corydon, Harrison County, Indiana.
- Graduated from the Indiana Normal School (Danville, Indiana).
- Read law in Jeffersonville, Clark County, Indiana, with James K. Marsh, a future judge of the Clark Circuit Court, from 1881 to 1883.
- Admitted to the bar in 1883.
- Began the practice of law in Clark County, Indiana.
- Elected to the Indiana General Assembly as Senator for Clark and Jefferson Counties in 1895 and 1897.
- Elected judge to the Indiana Appellate Court in 1906, serving until 1911.
- Practiced law in Indianapolis from 1911 to 1931.
- Died September 19, 1932, in Charlestown, Clark County, Indiana.

In Memoriam

JUDGE WARD H. WATSON

(Data Furnished by E. Prescott Long, Jeffersonville, Indiana)

Ward H. Watson was born November 7, 1859, on a farm near Corydon, Harrison County, Indiana. He was the son of Ward F. Watson and Mary M. (Smoot) Watson. He died at his home in Charlestown, Clark County, Indiana, on the 19th day of September, 1932.

His boyhood was spent on the farm where he was born. He attended the local schools and later completed his education at the Normal School at Danville, Indiana. When he became of age, he took up his residence at Charlestown, where for several years he taught school.

He then studied law in the office of James K. Marsh and with whom he was associated until Mr. Marsh became judge of the Clark Circuit Court.

Judge Watson was admitted to the bar in 1883 and practiced his profession in Clark County until 1906 when he was elected to the State Senate from Clark and Jefferson counties.

He was elected Judge of the Appellate Court of Indiana in 1906, and served for four years. He was a man of deep insight and was always reluctant to decide matters until they had been thoroughly discussed. His opinions are therefore highly valued, and it may be truthfully said that he had an important part in guiding the destinies of this great state.

In politics he was associated with A. T. Hert, James E. Watson, Albert J. Beveridge, John Sharp and others, in the guidance of the Republican Party in Indiana during the active years of his life.

(xxxii)

In 1918 Judge Watson built a beautiful home on the grounds formerly occupied by Johnathan Jennings, first governor of Indiana, which remains one of the finest homes in that locality.

On January 15, 1890, Judge Watson was married to Miss Edith R. Barnett of Charlestown, who died on January 29, 1910. He felt the loss of his wife most keenly and in her memory kept the home in which she died unoccupied, and in the same manner as it was at the time of her death.

Judge Watson was always interested in higher education and was at one time a trustee of Moores Hill College and was for a time President of the Board of Trustees of that institution.

After his term as Judge of the Appellate Court of Indiana had expired, he practiced law in Indianapolis until 1931, when he returned to his home in Charlestown, which he had maintained during all the years of his life he had been absent.

With the death of Judge Watson passes one of the most picturesque and lovable characters in Indiana political life.

Judge Watson leaves no children to carry on the good work started by him, but his friends and admirers, who looked to him for an example, will no doubt complete the work left unfinished by him.

Reprinted with permission from *Indiana Law Journal.* Vol. 6, 1930-1931
(Bloomington, Ind.: Indiana State Bar Association), facing p. 502.

William W. Miller
⌒ 1877-1931 ⌒

- Born January 3, 1877, in Nappanee, Elkhart County, Indiana.

- Taught school in Nappanee, Indiana.

- Moved to Denver, Colorado, to attend the University of Denver.

- Moved to Gary, Lake County, Indiana, in 1910.

- Became president of the Gary (Indiana) Bar Association.

- Elected to the Board of Managers for the Indiana State Bar Association in 1928.

- Became president of the Indiana State Bar Association in 1930.

- Died May 22, 1931, in Gary, Lake County, Indiana.

In Memoriam

William W. Miller

At a joint session of the Supreme and Appellate Courts upon July 1, 1931, Mr. Homer E. Sackett submitted the following: "I wish to respectfully suggest to these Courts the death of the Hon. William W. Miller, who died at his home in Gary, Indiana, on the 22nd day of March, 1931. At a meeting of the Gary Bar Association held in Gary on the 23rd day of May, 1931, a Memorial was adopted commemorative of the deceased and it is the desire of that association that the same be entered on the records of these Courts and published as a Memorial in a volume of decisions."

"The members of the Gary Bar Association mourn the death of their friend and brother member William W. Miller, and desire to pay tribute to his memory in grateful recognition of his untiring efforts directed toward the betterment of the profession and raising the standard of legal ethics throughout the state.

"The early experiences of Mr. Miller as a lawyer were in no respect different from other beginners. He came to Gary in the early days of his practice and started alone, with no money, no friends, no experience and no connections. The first years were hard and discouraging but with incessant work, industry and fair dealings, he gradually acquired a clientele which included many of the leading citizens of the community, whose constant return to his office for advice bespoke the confidence they reposed in him.

"For a number of years he has been known not only as one of the foremost lawyers of the county but also as a man who loved and believed in his profession. No remark derogatory of the legal profession, whether made by layman or lawyer, ever went unchallenged. He first attracted attention with regard to his efforts and desire to raise the standard of the profession when he became president of the Gary Bar Association, which office he held for a period of four years. Because of his splendid service rendered to his local association he soon became known throughout the State and his activities were brought to the attention of the Indiana State Bar Association. In 1928 he was elected as a member of the Board of Managers. The following year he was made vice-presi-

(xxvi)

dent and at the annual session in 1930 was raised to the high office of president, which position, the highest honor in the gift of the members of his profession, he filled with honor and credit to himself and the association till the time of his death. We who were in close touch with him know that he left unfinished some of his greatest ambitions in connection with this position. He had many plans for the betterment of the service of the association to the members of the bar. The endowment of the Indiana Law Journal, so as to assure its perpetuation, was one of his plans. His confidence in the worthiness and practicability of this plan overcame all obstacles and won for it the support of the Board of Managers. It is hoped that this plan may be carried on to completion and that the same may stand as a Memorial to the one who proposed and nurtured it.

"As a husband and father, he was devoted to his family and his chief recreation, after his long and strenuous day spent in the performance of his many activities, was in the sanctuary of his home with his wife and children about him.

"It is common knowledge that his greatest fault was overwork; that he never learned to play in the modern sense of the term; that overwork, as a result of his public spirited efforts to serve his profession, contributed materially to hasten the day of his death. It is fit that the death of such a citizen should be marked with all the testimonials of public grief, in order that his life may have its just influence on mankind; and while we deeply deplore the death of our friend and associate, we rejoice in the completeness of his life and labors, which, closing together, have left behind them a memory so precious.

> FRANK N. GAVIT,
> ORA L. WILDERMUTH,
> WILLIAM F. HODGES,
> ROBERT M. DAVIS,
> HOMER E. SACKETT.

At the request of the Chief Justice of the Supreme Court, Clarence R. Martin, and the Chief Justice of the Appellate Court, Harvey J. Curtis, a member of the Gary Bar Association, who responded with a high tribute to the life and work of Mr. Miller, and with the approval of the associate judges, the above was ordered spread upon the records of the Courts and published in a volume of the reports.

[REPORTER'S NOTE: The above Memoriam was submitted to the Reporter from the Clerk's office for publication January 4, 1937.]

Leonard J. Hackney
1855-1938

- Born March 29, 1855, in Edinburgh, Johnson County, Indiana.
- Received very little public school education.
- Employed in the law office of Hord & Blair in Shelbyville, Shelby County, Indiana, in 1871, and later became an assistant.
- Employed in the law office of John W. Kern in Kokomo, Howard County, Indiana, from 1873 to 1874.
- Became a clerk in the law firm of Baker, Hord, & Hendricks in Indianapolis, Marion County, Indiana, and studied law there.
- Returned to Shelbyville, Indiana, in 1876, and opened a law office.
- Elected prosecuting attorney of the Sixteenth Indiana Judicial Circuit for one term in 1878.
- Became judge of the Sixteenth Indiana Circuit Court on November 17, 1888.
- Elected to the Indiana Supreme Court in 1892, serving from January 2, 1893, until January 2, 1899.
- Became an attorney for the Cleveland, Cincinnati, Chicago & St. Louis Railway Company in 1905.
- Died October 3, 1938, in Winter Park, Florida.

In Memoriam

Leonard J. Hackney

Leonard J. Hackney was born to humble parents in Edinburg, Johnson County, Indiana, March 29, 1855. His opportunities for a school education were limited to five years in the common schools in the community in which he was born. At the early age of seventeen years, he began the study of law in the office of Hord and Blair, Attorneys in Shelbyville, Indiana. After spending approximately two years in his studies in Shelbyville, he first began to practice his profession at Kokomo, Indiana, in partnership with the Honorable John W. Kern, but after a few months in Kokomo, he moved to the City of Indianapolis, entering the law offices of Baker, Hord and Hendricks, one of the leading law firms of Indianapolis at that time. Here he remained until the year 1876, at which time he returned to the City of Shelbyville and formed a partnership with Isaac Odell for the practice of law. This partnership continued until 1879 when Mr. Hackney formed a partnership with Oliver J. Glessner and Edward K. Adams, of Shelbyville, which partnership continued until 1883, when Mr. Hackney formed a separate partnership with Mr. Adams under the name of Adams and Hackney.

In 1878 Judge Hackney was elected to the office of prosecuting attorney in the Judicial Circuit composed of Shelby and Johnson Counties, and in the year 1888 he was elected to the office of Judge in the same Circuit. In the year 1892 Judge Hackney was elected a member of the Supreme Court of the State of Indiana, in which office he served one full term, winning for himself distinguished honor and reputation as a jurist. Judge Hackney was nominated by his party for re-election in the year 1898, but before election time, he withdrew from the ticket and thereafter accepted a position of Assistant in the office of John T. Dye, General Counsel for the Cleveland, Cincinnati, Chicago & St. Louis Railway Company at Indianapolis, Indiana, and afterward became general counsel of the same company with offices in the City of Cincinnati, Ohio, which position he held with conspicuous ability until his retirement a few years ago. After his retirement, he moved to

(xx)

Winter Park, in the State of Florida, where he lived until his death, which occurred on the 2nd day of October in the year 1938.

Judge Hackney's span of life covered the period of most remarkable development of our country. He was an outstanding representative of the older members of the bar who attained high standing in and reflected credit on his profession without the advantages of early education and training. Unaided by early advantages he worked out his own way, winning distinction, credit, and honor for himself and his profession, and the pleasure of a quiet, peaceful, and honorable old age.

DAVID SMITH,
GEO. H. MEIKS,
EVERET E. STROUP,

Committee.

Memorial to Hon. Leonard J. Hackney, a member of this Court from 1893 to 1898, ordered spread of record in the order book of this Court and published in the official reports.

Dated this 20th day of December, 1938.

TREMAIN, C. J.

John Wesley Spencer
⌐ 1864-1939 ⌐

- Born March 7, 1864, at Mount Vernon, Wabash County, Indiana.
- Graduated from Mount Vernon High School in 1880.
- Studied at Central Indiana Normal (now Canterbury) College (Danville, Indiana) for one year, then studied law in his father's law office in Mount Vernon.
- Admitted to the Indiana bar on his twenty-first birthday.
- Practiced law in Mount Vernon until 1890.
- Elected prosecuting attorney of the First Indiana Judicial Circuit in 1890.
- Moved to Evansville, Vanderburgh County, Indiana in 1891.
- Re-elected prosecuting attorney in 1892 and remained in this post until 1895.
- Affiliated with the firm of Spencer & Brill until his appointment to the Vanderburgh Circuit Court in 1911.
- Elected to the Indiana Supreme Court and served from April 15, 1912, to January 17, 1918.
- Died June 28, 1939, in Madison, Wisconsin.

John W. Spencer

It is the desire of the court to pause and notice the passing of one who served with distinction as a member of the court, and to take cognizance of a resolution adopted by the bar of the county in which he practiced and made his home.

The resolution is as follows:

RESOLUTION OF VANDERBURGH COUNTY BAR ASSOCIATION UPON THE DEATH OF JUDGE JOHN W. SPENCER, SR., JUNE 30, 1939.

Judge John W. Spencer, Sr., lived from March 7, 1864, to June 28, 1939—seventy-five years full of- contacts that developed and strengthened and experiences which equipped for service of superior quality.

He was a man of deep-set convictions and determination at all times, and in whatever cause he rendered the maximum of service of mind and soul. These qualities were not accidental nor altogether acquired. He was born at a troubled period, of parents both strong, forceful and determined. By inheritance and early ambition he was destined for the law and was the middle member of three generations of lawyers of recognized and outstanding ability.

On March 7, 1885, his twenty-first birthday, he was admitted to the Bar of his native County of Posey, where he practiced five years before his election to the office of Prosecuting Attorney of the old First Judicial District composed of Vanderburgh and Posey Counties, and moved to Evansville, continuing in office four years, giving to the discharge of his duties his best. Thereafter, he and his partner, John R. Brill, built up a very large and lucrative practice until 1911 when he was appointed Judge of the Vanderburgh Circuit Court and in 1912 Judge of the Indiana Supreme Court. His elevation to the judgeship of Vanderburgh Circuit Court was to finish the unexpired term of Judge Curran A. DeBruler of sainted memory, and to the Supreme Court occasioned by the death of Judge James H. Jordan, after which he was elected to a six year term as Judge of the Indiana Supreme Court, becoming its Chief Justice. He succeeded Judges of rare ability and they were followed by a most worthy successor.

(xxii)

Judge Spencer was a man of extreme physical strength and mental power. His entrance into any presence was not a mere passing moment, but carried with it the immediate attention of all present—a feeling of security to those associated with him—of fear and trembling to those he opposed. He was a born advocate, logical and forceful, centering his powers of argument and persuasion on the underlying fundamental questions of right and wrong—of equity and fairness—more than to the cold technical questions of law involved.

In 1935, when he had concluded fifty years of active practice and service upon the bench, lauditory resolutions were passed by the bars of both Posey and Vanderburgh Counties.

Toward young men his attitude was of helpfulness, always impressing them with the idea of loyalty to cause and client. This loyalty was his life, and no man exceeded him in the devotion and in the force and determination to render of himself the best he had and of which he was capable.

He was a devotee of the majesty of the law and of the sanctity and dignity of the courts. His court room decorum can well be emulated by lawyers young and old. He never addressed the court sitting. As a practicing lawyer he had a profound respect for the position of the Judge and himself carried dignity to the bench always.

His passing leaves some of us many recollections of personal contacts fraught with significant meaning and memories which will continue to gladden and encourage. He lived longer than his years and "he fought a good fight."

Respectfully submitted,
EDGAR DURRE,
PHELPS F. DARBY,
WALTON M. WHEELER,
DANIEL H. ORTMEYER,
WILBUR C. CLIPPINGER,
FRANK H. HATFIELD, Chairman,
Committee.

The above and foregoing is ordered spread upon the records of this court as of this date, and published in the next volume of the reports of the decisions of this court.

Dated this 20th day of October, 1939.

MICHAEL L. FANSLER,
Chief Justice.

(xxiii)

Benjamin Milton Willoughby

～ 1855-1940 ～

- Born April 8, 1855, in Ripley County, Indiana.

- Graduated from high school in Vincennes, Knox County, Indiana, in 1876.

- Received an LL.B. from Cincinnati College (now the University of Cincinnati) in 1879 and was admitted to the bar that same year.

- Elected as an Indiana State Representative from 1895 to 1899.

- Served as judge for the Twelfth Circuit from 1912 to 1918.

- Served on the Indiana Supreme Court from January 6, 1919, to January 7, 1931.

- Died June 29, 1940, in Vincennes, Knox County, Indiana.

In Memoriam

Benjamin M. Willoughby
1855 = 1940

Benjamin Milton Willoughby was born in Ripley County, Indiana, May 8, 1855, the son of Milton and Phoebe (Osborn) Willoughby. He received his preparatory education at Vincennes, Indiana, completing the high school course in 1876. In 1879 he was graduated from the law department of Cincinnati college (now the University of Cincinnati) with the degree of LL.B.

Judge Willoughby practiced law at Vincennes continuously from 1880 until his election to the bench in 1912. He served as deputy prosecuting attorney in 1887 and was county attorney during 1897 and 1898. He was a member of the house of representatives in the 59th, 60th and 61st General Assemblies, serving as speaker pro temp. on several occasions. From 1912 until 1918 Judge Willoughby was judge of the 12th judicial circuit of Indiana. In 1919 and again in 1925 he was elected to the Supreme Court of Indiana. He retired from the bench to his home in Vincennes in 1931.

Judge Willoughby was a member of the Episcopal church and the Masonic Order. In politics, he was a Republican. He was the first president of the Knox County Bar Association. He married Edith Getches of Paoli, Indiana on July 8, 1912 and died without issue in Vincennes June 29, 1940. He was a courageous judge, a public-spirited citizen, a loyal friend and a devoted husband.

ORDER

It is ordered by the court that the foregoing memorial to the late Benjamin M. Willoughby be published in the official reports.

Dated this 19th day of February, 1942.

CURTIS G. SHAKE,
Chief Justice

(xxv)

Walter Emanuel Treanor

1883-1941

- Born November 17, 1883, in Loogootee, Martin County, Indiana.

- Received his education from Indiana University: a bachelor's degree, with honors (1912), a bachelor of laws degree (1922) and a doctorate of jurisprudence degree (1923).

- Earned a doctor of juridical science from Harvard University in 1927.

- Worked as a teacher and administrator in the Petersburg, Indiana public schools for thirteen years.

- Served as a second lieutenant in the United States Army during World War I.

- Taught law at Indiana University School of Law—Bloomington from 1922 to 1930.

- Was editor of the *Indiana Law Journal* from 1927 to 1930.

- Elected to the Indiana Supreme Court in 1930 and re-elected for a second term in 1936, serving from January 8, 1931, to December 27, 1937.

- Appointed to the United States Court of Appeals for the Seventh Circuit on December 27, 1937, where he served until his death.

- Died April 26, 1941, in Indianapolis, Marion County, Indiana.

Walter E. Treanor
1883 = 1941

The undersigned committee reports the following memorial for Judge Walter E. Treanor, who was a judge of this court from January, 1931, to 1936.

Walter E. Treanor was born at Loogootee, Indiana, on November 17, 1883, the son of James Donnelly Treanor and Gertrude Sommers Treanor. He was married to Aline Elizabeth Jean of Petersburg, Indiana, on December 9, 1916, who together with their one daughter, Rosemary, survives Judge Treanor.

He was graduated with honors from Indiana University with the degree of A.B. in 1912 and later received the degree of LL.B. and J.D., each with distinction, from Indiana University and the degree of S.J.D. from Harvard University. Prior to the World War, Judge Treanor was engaged in teaching in the public schools at Petersburg, Indiana, being the principal of the high school at that place from 1912 to 1915 and Superintendent of Schools from 1915 to 1917, at which latter date he enlisted and served overseas with the rank of lieutenant. At the end of the war he entered law school and received his LL.B. degree in 1922, his J.D. in 1923. He was professor of law at Indiana University School of Law from 1922 to 1930, having a leave of absence during the school year of 1926-1927 during which time he pursued his studies at Harvard and received the S.J.D. degree in 1927.

From 1927 to 1930 he was editor of the Indiana Law Journal. In 1930 he was elected Judge of the Supreme Court of Indiana and was re-elected in 1936, serving until his appointment as Judge of the United States Circuit Court of Appeals (Seventh Circuit), which position he occupied until his death on April 26, 1941.

Judge Treanor was a member of the American, Indiana and Monroe County Bar Associations, Phi Beta Kappa, Delta Sigma Rho, Gamma Eta Gamma, and the Order of Coif.

To his associates on the bench and his many friends at the bar and in private life, Judge Treanor will be remembered for his kindly and cheerful disposition, his

(xxvi)

sense of humor, his fine scholarship and his devotion to justice.

ALFRED EVENS,
JOHN P. O'DONNELL,
DONALD A. ROGERS,

Committee of the
Monroe County Bar

ORDER

It is ordered by the court that the foregoing memorial to the late Walter E. Treanor be published in the official reports.

Dated this 24th day of February, 1942.

CURTIS G. SHAKE,
Chief Justice

Howard L. Townsend

~ 1870-1950 ~

- Born in 1870 near Eaton, Ohio.

- Moved with his family from Ohio to Angola, Steuben County, Indiana, where he attended high school.

- Earned a bachelor's degree from Bethany College (Bethany, West Virginia).

- Returned to Angola to teach Greek, Latin, and Mathematics.

- Enrolled at the Chicago Kent College of Law after teaching for a few years.

- Returned to Indiana and practiced law in Fort Wayne, Allen County, Indiana, from 1904 onward.

- Served on the Indiana Supreme Court from October 5, 1917, to November 1, 1923.

- Was very active in Republican politics.

- Well-known for his love of literature and poetry.

- Died March 20, 1950, in Florida.

In Memoriam

Howard L. Townsend
1870-1950

Howard L. Townsend was born on a farm near Eaton, Ohio, in the year 1870, and died a resident of Fort Wayne, Indiana, on March 20, 1950. He graduated from the Angola, Indiana, High School and Bethany College, in West Virginia, where he received an A.B. degree.

He taught Greek, Latin, and mathematics at Tri-State College in Angola. Thence he went to Chicago and studied at the Chicago Kent College of Law, from which he received an L.L.B. degree.

For awhile he practiced law in Chicago. In 1904 he came to Fort Wayne. There he was associated in the practice with Newton W. Gilbert, who became Vice-Governor of the Philippine Islands, and with Sol A. Wood, who later became Judge of the Circuit Court of Allen County.

From 1917 to 1923 Howard L. Townsend was a member of the Supreme Court of Indiana. He succeeded Richard Erwin, who had died. He was elected to a full six-year term. After this judgeship, Judge Townsend resumed the practice of law in Fort Wayne.

This renowned member of this Bar was the quintessence of intellectuality, not only in the field of law, but in the field of life. He exemplified the rightful concept of the lawyer as one well versed in other subjects. He continued to teach himself the classics of literature. He was an astute student of Shakespeare. His favorite poet was Burns. He loved Mark Twain.

lxxvi

IN MEMORIAM lxxvii

One of his favorite poems was "The Last Leaf" by Oliver Wendell Holmes. A verse therefrom is:

"They say that in his prime,
Ere the pruning knife of time cut him down,
Not a better man was found
By the Crier on his round
Through the town."

At the age of almost four score, Judge Townsend, like the last leaf on the tree, was strong and in his intellectual prime.

Judge Townsend wrote some classics himself. We refer to his opinions as Judge of the State Supreme Court.

His opinions were sharp, thorough, concise, concerned with the essentialities of the case, the merits. They are masterpieces in clarity and pointedness of expression. His erudition was transcribed into his decisions.

He was a profound thinker. He took his thinking straight, unimpeded by emotionalism. With him competence was an obsession. He displayed impatience with laxity and intellectual laziness. One should find the law one's self and not ascertain it by parasitical means, was a practiced precept.

Judge Townsend was rather complete unto himself. He was self-reliant and fully self-confident. Even so, he had the means wherewith to fashion accomplishment.

He carried efficiency to the details of life. Everything, not just books, not just law, had to be thoroughly understood in the minutest details.

While he shall be greatly missed by the members of the Bar and of this Court, he perpetuates himself through notable decisions made while a member of this Court.

lxxviii   IN MEMORIAM

                          ORDER

   It is ordered by the court that the foregoing memorial
to the late Howard L. Townsend be published in the
official reports.

   Dated this 3rd day of April, 1950.

                              PAUL G. JASPER,
                              Chief Justice.

George Lee Tremain
1874-1948

- Born April 6, 1874, near Hartsville, Bartholomew County, Indiana.

- Received an elementary education in county schools and entered Central Normal (now Canterbury) College in Danville, Hendricks County, Indiana, in 1894.

- Taught school from 1895 to 1898.

- Re-entered Central Normal College for the 1898-99 term.

- Graduated from the Indiana Law School in Indianapolis in 1900.

- Began practicing law in Greensburg, Decatur County, Indiana, in 1901, in association with Judge James K. Ewing.

- Formed a partnership with Rollin A. Turner in 1907, specializing in criminal law.

- Elected to the Indiana Supreme Court, serving from January 1, 1935, until December 31, 1940.

- Returned to the practice of law in Greensburg in 1941.

- Died February 8, 1948, in Greensburg, Decatur County, Indiana.

In Memoriam

George L. Tremain
1874 = 1948

It is with a sense of profound sorrow that the members of the Decatur County Bar Association meet with the members of the adjoining Bar Associations for the purpose of paying their respects to the memory of the late George L. Tremain.

George L. Tremain, aged 73, passed away at his home at 8 P. M. Sunday, February 8th. He was born in Bartholomew County near Hartsville, April 6, 1874, the son of John W. and Eliza Jones Tremain. His youth was spent in Jackson Township in Decatur County, Indiana, where he received his early education at Alert and other schools in the township and where he made friendships which endured throughout his entire lifetime and it is only fair in passing to say that he had the deepest affection for the memories of his boyhood friends and of his early life in Jackson Township.

In 1894 he entered Central Normal College at Danville now known as Canterbury College. He taught school for a time and then attended Indiana Law School at Indianapolis for a short period and reentered Central Normal College at Danville and completed his formal education in 1900.

He entered the law practice in Greensburg, Indiana, in 1901 by forming a partnership with the late James K. Ewing. In 1907, he and the late Rollin A. Turner formed a law partnership under the firm name of Tremain and Turner which firm was to become one of the outstanding law firms in this section of Indiana.

xlii

In June 1934, Judge Tremain was nominated for the office of Judge of the Indiana Supreme Court and was elected to that office in November of that year.

By political affiliation he was a Democrat but he never regarded himself as a politician, and the decisions which he rendered on the Supreme Court bore out the fact that his principal responsibility to the litigants before him was the intelligent application of the principles of the law based upon justice and equity. The law profession to him was one which placed upon the shoulders of the representatives of that profession the utmost responsibility to render service honestly, fairly and ethically.

After Judge Tremain left the bench, he formed a partnership in Greensburg in his old office with William L. Woodfill and John W. Goddard, and the partnership continued in the practice until 1947 when Mr. Goddard was elected Judge of the Decatur Circuit Court.

He was an active member in the affairs of the Indiana State Bar Association, served several years as a member of the Board of Managers of the State Association and he was a member of the American Bar Association. His civic activities were connected with the Greensburg Lodge No. 36 F. & A. M. and the Greensburg Elks Club No. 475. He has been for many years an active director of the Union Trust Company of Greensburg and was president of the Greensburg Times Company and was an honorary member of the legal fraternity of Phi Delta Phi at Indiana University.

He was married to his surviving widow, Mary Littell, on September 27, 1910. He is also survived by a brother, Dr. M. A. Tremain of Adams and a sister, Mrs. S. F. Stewart of Richmond, Indiana, and by several nieces and nephews.

In every way he upheld the best traditions of the bench and bar and his opinions were received with the greatest respect by his fellow lawyers and judges.

His conduct and bearing were an example to the younger members of the Bar whom he always treated with the greatest kindness and to whom he was always eager to lend the benefit of his counsel. It can be said to his credit that he was always interested in the welfare of all young people and was always willing to lend a helping hand and particularly to any young lawyer just beginning the practice.

As a practicing attorney he was studious, careful, painstaking and honest, always respectful and courteous to both the court and opposing counsel.

THEREFORE, be it now resolved by the members of the Decatur County Bar Association of Indiana in a special Memorial Meeting held at the Court House in Greensburg, Indiana, that in the passing of the mortal life of Judge George L. Tremain that this Association and the bench and bar of Indiana have lost an efficient, helpful and industrious lawyer and jurist and that the citizens of this community and of this state have lost a dependable and resourceful public servant.

*   *   *

Respectfully submitted,
Edgar E. Hite,
John W. Goddard,
Hugh D. Wickens,
Committee.

David A. Myers,
President Decatur County
Bar Association.

ORDER

It is ordered by the court that the foregoing memorial to the late George L. Tremain be published in the official reports.

Dated this 12th day of April, 1949.

OLIVER STARR,
Chief Justice.

xliv

Louis B. Ewbank

⌒ 1864-1953 ⌒

- Born September 5, 1864, in Guilford, Dearborn County, Indiana.

- Educated in the Dearborn County schools and studied law in the offices of William Watson Woollen, beginning in 1891.

- Practiced law in the firm of Hanan, Ewbank, & Hanana in LaGrange, LaGrange County, Indiana, from 1910 to 1912, then moved to Indianapolis.

- Elected Marion County Circuit Court judge in 1914.

- Appointed to the Indiana Supreme Court in 1920 by Governor James P. Goodrich, filling the vacancy created by the death of Justice Harvey.

- Elected for a six-year term in the Indiana Supreme Court, serving from January 1, 1920, until January 3, 1927.

- Returned to private practice at Whitcomb, Ewbank, & Dowden in 1927.

Continued ⌒

Louis B. Ewbank

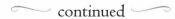

continued

- Entered a law practice with his brother, Richard L. Ewbank, in 1940.

- Served on the faculty of the Indiana Law School (Indianapolis) from 1897 to 1914, and lectured at the Indiana University School of Law—Bloomington.

- Noted for writing the following publications: *Manual of Indiana Appellate Practice; Indiana Trial Practice; Indiana Criminal Law* (also known as "the prosecutor's Bible"); and *Indiana Cumulative Digest* (editor from 1904-1914).

- Died March 6, 1953, in Guilford, Dearborn County, Indiana.

In Memoriam

Louis B. Ewbank
1864-1953

Louis Blasdel Ewbank, 88, former member of the Supreme Court of Indiana, former judge of Marion Circuit Court, and prominent member of the bar of the City of Indianapolis, passed away at the Ewbank Homestead at Guilford, Indiana, March 7, 1953.

Judge Ewbank was a member of a pioneer family which entered the Indiana Territory in 1811, settling in what is now Dearborn county, on Tanner's Creek. His great-grandparents came down the Ohio River by flatboat, bringing with them their few belongings, to carve out a home in the wilderness. In 1828 the family homestead was erected. There Judge Ewbank, one of ten children of John W. and Betsey Blasdel Ewbank, was born on September 5, 1864. There, also, he spent his boyhood days, and there he died.

His brief formal education was confined to the rural schools of that day. He helped with the farm tasks, and as he grew to young manhood, decided to teach school. For a time he taught rural schools in Dearborn county, at Dillsboro and at Aurora. His interest then turned to the law, and he studied for a short time in law offices in Lawrenceburg.

In 1891, he came to Indianapolis, to read law in the office of William W. Woolen, a noted lawyer of his day. Later, he associated in the practice of law with Benjamin F. Watson, a noted law editor and author, late of the Indianapolis bar, and for several years, they maintained offices where the Kresge Building now

(xliv)

stands, at Washington and Pennsylvania Streets. In 1893, he married Effie Shoemaker, a schoolteacher at Broad Ripple, Indiana. She died in 1901. They had no children.

As a young lawyer, he took up the teaching of law in the Indiana Law School at Indianapolis, and devoted considerable energy to law writing. For a period of several years, he edited the Indiana Cumulative Digest, and did the court work for the newspapers, digesting the opinions of the Supreme and Appellate Courts. During these early years he authored three books, Ewbank's Trial Evidence, Ewbank's Manual of Practice, and Ewbank's Indiana Criminal Law, in addition to writing for various legal periodicals. Many of the lawyers throughout the state, remember him best as a teacher of law. It was from the Indiana Law School, that he received his only degree, an honorary LLB degree.

In 1909, his brother, Richard L. Ewbank, moved to Indianapolis from Mason City, Iowa, to join with Judge Ewbank in maintaining his law office and practice at Indianapolis, while he became associated in an extensive railroad practice with the law firm of Hanan, Ewbank and Hanan, at LaGrange, Indiana.

In 1914, Louis Ewbank was elected judge of the Marion Circuit Court. While a judge of that court, he decided many important cases. He unsuccessfully sought nomination for Supreme Court Judge in 1918. Upon the death of Lawson M. Harvey, he was appointed to the Supreme Court of Indiana, by Governor James Goodrich. Shortly thereafter he was elected to succeed himself on the Supreme Court bench.

He served with distinction as a member of the state's highest tribunal until January, 1927, when his term expired. As a judge of the Circuit Court, not only were his decisions sound and eminently fair, but the bar of the period from 1914 to 1920, also remember him best

(xlv)

for his patience and understanding of the problems confronting the young lawyer. His opinions written while a member of the Supreme Court of Indiana were always clearly and frankly stated, and based upon solid legal reasoning and extensive research. Many times he read far into the night in his legal researches, to produce an opinion exhaustive of the questions presented by the case. Many of his opinions serve as leading precedents today.

During the Harding administration, he was mentioned for a vacancy existing upon the Supreme Court of the United States, but did not receive the appointment.

After 12 years on the bench, he returned to the law practice in 1927. Soon he was presenting the legislative pay case for members of the 1927 State Legislature. He joined the law firm of Shirley, Whitcomb and Dowden, which became known as Whitcomb, Ewbank and Dowden, and later Ewbank and Dowden.

In 1940, he rejoined his brother, with offices in the State Life Building. This association lasted until the death of Richard L. Ewbank in December, 1947. Later he practiced with his nephew, Albert W. Ewbank, until illness forced his retirement.

No young lawyer commencing practice was ever turned away by Judge Ewbank, who was always ready to give good and kindly counsel. He had a sympathetic understanding of their problems and struggles, and often gave financial assistance to worthy beginners.

For many years he taught and lectured at the Indiana Law School, and served as a member of its Board of Trustees. He also lectured at the Indiana University School of Law at Bloomington, Indiana.

An active Republican, he maintained a lively interest in civic and political affairs of the community.

He was a member of the Mystic Tie Lodge, F. & A. M. and would have completed 50 years membership this year. He held membership in the York and Scottish

Rite bodies of Masonry, and the Murat Shrine. For
many years, he took an active part in the degree work
of the Masons. He also held many positions of prominence in the affairs of the I. O. O. F. over a period of
more than 50 years. As a studious member of the Indiana Historical Society, he contributed numerous
papers to that organization. He also belonged to the
Indiana Society of Pioneers, the Sons of American
Revolution, the Columbia Club, the Indianapolis Literary Society, and the Century Club. For a number of
years, he actively participated in the affairs of the
American Law Institute and aided in drafting the Re-
statements of Law. He was a distinguished member of
the Indianapolis, Indiana State and American Bar
Associations.

He lived alone for many years, maintaining residence
at 614 North East Street, in Indianapolis for more than
43 years. He found both comfort and strength in his
many friends, and in his great love for the law. His
studies sustained him, not only as a deep student of the
law, but also as a pre-eminent law teacher and jurist.

He is survived by two brothers, James H. Ewbank, a
lawyer of Lawrenceburg, Indiana, and Loebo J. Ewbank,
and a sister, Elizabeth Hall, both of whom live at the
Ewbank Homestead.

Respectfully submitted,

HERMAN W. KOTHE,
EARL R. COX,
SHERWOOD BLUE,
ALBERT W. EWBANK,
B. HOWARD CAUGHRAN, *Chairman*
Memorial Committee,
Indianapolis Bar Association.

PAUL N. ROWE,
President of Indianapolis
Bar Association

(xlvii)

ORDER

It is hereby ordered by the court that the foregoing memorial to the late Louis B. Ewbank be published in the official reports of the Indiana Supreme Court.

Dated this *18th* day of June, 1953.

ARCH N. BOBBITT,
Chief Justice.

Frank Earl Gilkison

1877-1955

- Born November 3, 1877, in Martin County, Indiana.

- Received a law degree from Indiana University in 1901.

- Practiced law in Shoals, Martin County, Indiana from 1901 to 1935.

- Served as deputy prosecuting attorney in Shoals from 1907 to 1909.

- Served as a circuit court judge in the Forty-ninth Circuit from 1935 to 1945.

- Served on the Indiana Supreme Court from January 1, 1945, until his death.

- Died February 25, 1955, in Indianapolis, Marion County, Indiana.

In Memoriam

FRANK E. GILKISON

1877 - 1955

The undersigned committee, appointed by the President of the Daviess County Bar Association, submits the following memorial upon the life of the Honorable Frank E. Gilkison, a charter member of our Association:

The unrelenting and impartial hand of death has called from our ranks a great lawyer and judge. He died suddenly and quietly, while at breakfast, in Indianapolis, on February 25, 1955, at the age of seventy-seven. Our profession can ill afford to lose such an industrious and able lawyer and judge as our departed friend, Judge Gilkison.

Judge Gilkison was born in Rutherford Township, Martin County, Indiana, on March 3, 1877. The Gilkison family is of Scotch-English descent. His parents were John and Matilda (Inman) Gilkison. There were seven children in the family. Alva O. Gilkinson and James E. Gilkison, brothers, and Eva Gilkison, a sister, predeceased Judge Gilkison. Dr. John S. Gilkison and Dr. William L. Gilkison, brothers, are now residing in Martin County, Indiana, and a sister, Mrs. Cecil Parrish, resides at Speedway, Indiana.

Judge Gilkison as a young man married Daisy Kennedy, of Shoals, Indiana. She died at an early age. He later married Eva Edwards, of Washington, Indiana,

(xliii)

on June 17, 1925. She survives him. They have one son, Frank E. Gilkison, Jr. He married Barbara Black, of Washington, Indiana. Frank practices law in Muncie, Indiana, with the firm of White and Haymond. Judge and Mrs. Gilkison have two grandchildren.

Judge Gilkison attended Indiana University, receiving his LLB in 1901. He was elected to two terms as Judge of the Daviess Circuit Court, beginning his first term in 1934, and serving until he was elected Judge of the Supreme Court of Indiana in 1944. He went on the bench of the Supreme Court of Indiana in 1945, which position he filled until his death, at which time he was its Chief Justice.

Judge Gilkison was a member of the Methodist Church, most of the Masonic Orders, the Elks, Moose, Rotary, and Columbia Club.

Judge Gilkison practiced for many years in most of the Circuit Courts of Southern Indiana. He started practicing law at Shoals, Indiana, and entered into a partnership with Hiram Mc Cormick. This partnership was of short duration, and after that Judge Gilkison always practiced alone. He was an active trial lawyer, and had a natural love for the courtroom contest. He was a lawyer's lawyer. He was never known to pick and choose his clients and cases, to avoid controversy or courtroom battles. The weak and the poor could seek and gain his services. He was extremely well-schooled in trial tactics, and it was interesting to hear him relate his courtroom experiences from a long career of trial practice.

Judge Gilkison ran true to form of the tradition of the Circuit trial lawyer, in that he had a good literary background, knew the Bible well, and had a deep compassion for and appreciation of the human being. A comprehensive knowledge of constitutional law is indispensable to a lawyer or a judge who has a proper regard for his profession. Judge Gilkison was a fine

(xliv)

student of constitutional law, both State and Federal. He was a cool, competitive adversary. He never neglected his client because of indolence, apathy, or inattention to his business. There appeared in his nature and character an unmistakable thread of kindness, and a sincere warmth of personality.

Judge Gilkison was individualistic in his thinking, and had the courage of his convictions, legal and political. The fact that his opinion at the time would not be the most popular one did not deter him from expressing his position. He spoke out, in a day when it seems to be the tendency of even many of our intelligent people to rationalize the actions of everyone, and protest against none.

He adhered religiously to the principle of the dignity of the human being, and the inalienable rights of the individual. Any constitutional question that touched upon the rights and dignity of the human being aroused his careful consideration. His occasional dissenting opinion while on the Supreme Court proclaimed him to be a mental leader, and not a mere follower.

He was a dependable leader and faithful worker in the Republican party throughout his life. He believed that Americans should take care of America first.

As a judge and a lawyer, he was kind, helpful, and patient. He was particularly considerate of young lawyers.

Professionally, he had the high esteem of his professional brethren. This is a silent esteem among professionals, which proceeds from a cool, calculated and impartial estimation of the ability of a lawyer. This esteem cannot be artificially created. It is born of sharp contests, industry, and pure logic of the mind. It is also based on integrity, staunch character, skill, and devotion to duty. No subservient "yes-man" or mere manipulator or negotiator can secure it.

(xlv)

The esteem of lawyers among their professional brothers is slowly earned, but when once earned, it is a precious heritage. Judge Gilkison had that esteem.

As we extend to his dear wife, fine young son and relatives, our deepest sympathy, and our deep respect for a great lawyer and a great judge, we all are sobered in the knowledge that man, be he high or low, important or insignificant, in his true sense is a humble being, and that we must all be prepared for that humbling experience of death. We feel that Judge Gilkison, a humble man, was prepared for that experience.

Respectfully submitted this fourth day of May, 1955.

> (Signed) Philip D. Waller, CHAIRMAN
> F. A. Seal
> Arthur Allen
> Robert O. Chambers

The committee respectfully requests the Court that this Memorial be spread of record in the Civil Order Book of this Court.

It is therefore ordered by the Court that the foregoing Memorial to the late Frank E. Gilkison be spread in the Civil Order Book of this Court.

Dated this fourth day of May, 1955.

> (Signed) Philip D. Waller, Judge
> Daviess Circuit Court

The court orders the above Resolution spread of record on the Order Books of this court, and the Clerk of this Court is ordered to deliver a copy of said Resolution to the Reporter of this court, who is ordered to print and publish the same in the Indiana Reports.

Dated June 15, A.D., 1955.

> (Signed) James A. Emmert,
> Chief Justice.

(xlvi)

David Albert Myers

~ 1859-1955 ~

- Born August 5, 1859, in Cass County, Indiana.

- Attended Smithson College, Danville Normal College (Danville, Indiana), and Union University.

- Received a law degree from Union (now Albany) Law School (Albany, New York) in 1882.

- Began practicing law in Greensburg, Decatur County, Indiana, in 1883.

- Appointed judge of the Eighth Indiana Judicial District in 1899.

- Served as county prosecutor for the Decatur-Rush Judicial District in 1890 and 1892.

- Appointed judge of the First District Indiana Appellate Court, and then elected to the post, serving from 1904 until 1913.

- Elected to the Indiana Supreme Court in 1916, and re-elected in 1922 and 1928, serving from January 1, 1917, to December 31, 1934.

- Died July 1, 1955, in Greensburg, Decatur County, Indiana.

In Memoriam

DAVID A. MYERS
1859 - 1955

Judge David Albert Myers died at Greensburg, his home, July 1, 1955, aged 95 years.

He was born in Cass County, Indiana, August 5, 1859, on the home farm of his father and mother, Henry C. and Maria (Bright) Myers. His father was a native of Butler County, Ohio, and his mother was born in Virginia, both descendants of sturdy pioneer ancestors.

Judge Myers received his higher education at Smithson College, Danville Normal College, and Union University. In 1881 he was graduated from Albany Law School, and that year he moved to Greensburg and there began the practice of law.

He had a distinguished and honorable career in the public service, which gave him a wide experience and thorough understanding of public affairs, so well reflected in his many outstanding judicial opinions. In 1886 he was elected City Attorney of Greensburg, and in 1890 and 1892 was elected Prosecuting Attorney of the Decatur-Rush joint judicial circuit. In 1899, Governor Mount appointed him Judge of the 8th Judicial Circuit, then consisting of Bartholomew and Decatur Counties, and he served as trial judge until the next general election in 1900. On October 18, 1904, he was

(xlvii)

appointed Judge of the Appellate Court of Indiana from the First District, and in 1904 and 1908 he was elected to this court, and there served until January 1, 1913.

His judicial career was resumed in 1916, when he was elected Judge of the Supreme Court of Indiana, and in 1922 and 1928 he was again elected to that court, completing his eighteen years record there on December 31, 1934.

Judge Myers, by the opinions he wrote, and those in which he concurred, established an unexcelled record as a great judge. His opinions always disclosed careful research and skilled craftmanship, with logical reasoning well supported by many authorities. He had a vast knowledge of the rules to be invoked in statutory construction, and his philosophy of the public service never departed from the principle that public office is a public trust. His terms as Prosecuting Attorney never colored his opinions in criminal appeals, and no judge was ever more careful to protect the legal and constitutional rights of every citizen alike. If he ever erred it was in the cause of liberty and freedom. His opinions on constitutional questions were outstanding and have stood the test of time.

Judge Myers was always interested in public affairs in his home community and in the state. He was one of the Founding Fathers of the Indiana State Bar Association, and was a continuous member thereof until his death.

THEREFORE, BE IT RESOLVED, by the Tenth District Bar Association, in meeting assembled at New Castle, Indiana, this 8th day of July, A.D. 1955, that we do express our deep regret on the death of one of the great judges of the Appellate and Supreme Courts of Indiana, and that we do hereby publicly acknowledge the great debt of gratitude owed this distinguished and honored jurist by all the Bench and Bar of this State.

TENTH DISTRICT BAR ASSOCIATION

By (Signed)   Gustave H. Hoelscher
     ”   Herrod Carr
     ”   James H. Ronald
                          COMMITTEE

(Signed)   Malcolm M. Edwards, President
            Tenth District Bar Association
(Signed)   J. R. Hinshaw, Secretary

The above resolution is now ordered spread of record on the order books of the court, and the Clerk of the Court is ordered to deliver a copy thereof to the Reporter of this Court, who is directed to publish the same in the next official report of this court.

July 12, 1955.

(Signed)   James A. Emmert,
            Chief Justice

Frank Nelson Richman

⌒ 1881-1956 ⌒

- Born July 1, 1881, in Columbus, Bartholomew County, Indiana.

- Received a bachelor's degree from Lake Forest (Lake Forest, Illinois) College in 1904, and a law degree (J.D.) from the University of Chicago in 1909.

- Admitted to the Indiana bar in 1908.

- Served on the Indiana Supreme Court from January 6, 1941, to January 6, 1947.

- Taught at the Indiana University School of Law—Indianapolis beginning in 1944.

- Served as a judge of the American Military Tribunal, Division IV, Nuremberg Group in 1947.

- Served as chair of the Indiana Judicial Council.

- Died April 29, 1956, in Indianapolis, Marion County, Indiana.

In Memoriam

FRANK NELSON RICHMAN

1881-1956

The lives of great Americans are written in services— services to their communities, to their states, to their nation, and in all to their fellowmen. Judge Frank N. Richman measured high in all these categories. It is with deep sorrow that we mark his passing from his labors among us.

Judge Frank Nelson Richman died April 28, 1956, after six months of illness, at his home at 524 East 53rd Street, Indianapolis. He was seventy-four years of age.

Judge Richman was born July 1, 1881, at Columbus, Indiana, to Dr. Silas Tevis Richman, a physician, and Elma Baker Richman, and spent his early life in Columbus, Indiana, Princeton, Kansas, and Chicago, Illinois, at which places his father practiced medicine.

After graduating from high school he entered Northwestern university to study medicine, but after graduating from Lake Forest (Illinois) College in 1904, he turned to newspaper work and served on newspapers in Rockford, Illinois, and LaCrosse, Wisconsin.

Later he entered the University of Chicago Law School and completed his studies there and was admitted to the bar in 1908. The same year he returned to Columbus and entered a law partnership with his uncle, the late Judge Charles S. Baker. In 1931, when Mr. Baker became judge of the Bartholomew Circuit Court, Mr. Richman and Julian Sharpnack formed a law partnership

(xliv)

which continued until 1941. Judge Richman was elected to the Supreme Court of Indiana in 1940, entered upon his duties in 1941, and served until 1947.

In 1947, Judge Richman served as a judge on the American Tribunal IV in the International Court which tried German war criminals at Nuernberg, Germany.

Leaving the Supreme Court, Judge Richman became a professor of law at Indiana University Law School, having classes at both Bloomington and Indianapolis, and retiring in September, 1952, as a professor emeritus. He remained active, however, after his retirement. Being a specialist in labor relations law, he acted as arbitrator in several labor disputes. He also served as special judge in circuit courts in Indiana.

During his residence in Columbus, Judge Richman left a lasting impression upon the civic life of this city. He aided in establishing the Columbus Foundation for Youth and the Bartholomew County Historical Society. He was chairman of the Columbus Chapter of the American Red Cross from 1922 to 1939. He was one of the organizers of the Rotary Club of Columbus, and served as its president.

Judge Richman was a scholarly man, a good student of the law, and honesty and integrity were personal attributes that were at the foundation of his practice.

His professional affiliations included the American Bar Association, the American Judicature Society, the Indiana State Bar Association, and the Bartholomew County Bar Association. He was president of the State Bar Association in 1931 and 1932, and was chairman of legal education in 1930.

Judge Richman was a member of the Presbyterian Church. He was an elder in the First Presbyterian Church at Columbus, and later a member of the First Presbyterian Church of Indianapolis.

He was a member of the Phi Delta Phi legal fraternity, the Order of Coif, and the Columbia Club.

(xlv)

Judge Richman was married December 24, 1908, to Miss Edith Elizabeth Rogers. They became the parents of a son, Col. C. P. Richman, of Alexandria, Virginia, and three daughters, Mrs. Harold M. Coons of Indianapolis, Mrs. Bruce Johnson, of Oklahoma City, Oklahoma, and Mrs. John Heflin, of Indianapolis. He is survived by his widow, the four children, nine grandchildren, and a sister, Miss Alice Richman.

We extend our sympathies to his widow, his relatives and friends on behalf of the Bar of Bartholomew County.

Be It, Therefore, Resolved, by this the Bartholomew County Bar Association, that this our expression of sympathy and appreciation be spread upon the minutes of this meeting; that a copy thereof be sent to the family of our departed friend, Frank Nelson Richman, and that a copy thereof be offered for inclusion in the records of the Bartholomew Circuit Court.

(Signed)   John E. Summa
Julian Sharpnack
Charlton J. Walker
Committee on Resolutions.

Adopted by the Bartholomew County, Indiana, Bar Association, May 1, 1956.

(Signed)   Sidney H. Showalter, V.P.

The court orders the above Resolution spread of record on the Order Books of this court, and the Clerk of this court is ordered to deliver a copy of said Resolution to the Reporter of this court, who is ordered to print and publish the same in the Indiana Reports.
Dated May 7th, 1956.

(Signed)   Arch N. Bobbitt
Chief Justice

Hardses Nathan Swaim
1890-1957

- Born November 30, 1890, in Zionsville, Boone County, Indiana.

- Graduated from DePauw University (Greencastle, Indiana) in 1913.

- Received a law degree cum laude from the University of Chicago in 1916.

- Joined the United States Army in 1917, reaching the rank of first lieutenant with the 87th and the 88th Infantry Divisions during World War I.

- Began legal practice in Indianapolis, Marion County, Indiana, in 1916.

- Became active in Democratic politics, serving as Marion County Democratic chairman from 1930 to 1934, Twelfth District chairman from 1936 to 1938, and Indianapolis city controller from 1937 to 1938.

- Elected to the Indiana Supreme Court on the Democratic ticket in 1938, serving from January 1, 1939, to January 1, 1945.

- Appointed to the United States Seventh Circuit Court of Appeals in Chicago by President Truman in 1949, serving until his death.

- Died July 30, 1957, in Indianapolis, Marion County, Indiana.

In Memoriam

HARDSES NATHAN SWAIM
1890-1957

H. Nathan Swaim, the son of Charles R. and Alice Avery Swaim, was born at Zionsville, Indiana, November 30, 1890. Upon graduation from High School there he entered DePauw University, and was graduated in 1913. There he earned his way by waiting table in a campus cafe and as a tutor in German for other students. After teaching a year in the Zionsville High School, he entered the Chicago Law School and was graduated in 1916 with the Degree of Doctor of Jurisprudence *cum laude*, and elected as a member of the Order of Coif. At De-Pauw he was a Sigma Nu and at Chicago Law School a Phi Delta Phi.

He entered military service in 1917, and served as a First Lieutenant with the 88th and 87th Infantry Divisions, a branch of his own choice.

On July 14, 1917, he married Clara A. Renner of Rushville. Their two children are Robert W. Swaim and Norma Jean Swaim (now Nutter).

In the practice of law he first became associated with and then a partner of James N. Ogden, who is remembered for his outstanding leadership in the community, as a politician, a faithful church worker, a teacher, the Dean of the Law School in Indianapolis, a fine lecturer,

(xlviii)

and who with Mrs. Ogden organized and sponsored the Ogden Choir singers who sing at the Easter Sunrise Service each year.

Without money, financial backing, or wealthy social contacts, but rather on account of his industry, good health, legal training and warm affections, Nate Swaim soon became recognized as a capable practitioner and a lawyer's lawyer. He had the unusual ability of taking any set of facts in most any field and reducing those facts to legal issues promptly and accurately. He dedicated himself to study and public service in the true professional sense.

In Civic and Public Service before becoming a Judge, Nate Swaim was Commander of his Legion Post, a member of the Board of School Commissioners, President of the County Chapter of the National Foundation for Infantile Paralysis, Trustee of the Soldiers and Sailors Children's Home, Director of the Travelers Aid Society, Democratic County and District Chairman, City Controller, City Corporation Counsel and active in his Methodist hurch, the Y.M.C.A. and the Boy Scout affairs.

His steady hand, and the level, thoughtful head whose ingenuity together with an untiring effort won for him a countless number of warm and lasting friendships. His friends will long recall a Christian gentleman with a zest for the good life.

For recreation he was an ardent fisherman, spending his summers at Lake Freeman with his family. He liked to relate an experience with his six-year-old grandson while the two were fishing together. The grandson inquired, "Granddad, are you a judge *and* a fisherman?". To this grandfather nodded. Then after looking out over the water for a long time the grandson said, "I guess you are *more of a fisherman* than you are a judge." His loyalty and duty to family always came first. The home was one of kindness and genuine understanding.

(xlix)

He was elected and served as a Judge of our Indiana Supreme Court from 1939 to 1945. His opinions are easily understood, logically sound and legally supported. On November 7, 1949, he was appointed to the United States Circuit Court of Appeals for the Seventh Circuit in Chicago, and served with distinction until his death July 30, 1957.

Through the years of his professional life he was a member of our Indianapolis, Indiana and American Bar Associations. He will long be remembered for his superior deeds as a lawyer, the politician, the judge, the soldier, the citizen, the fisherman, the husband, the father, the churchman and the friend to his fellowman. The more one studies his life and accomplishments, the more one is impressed that his life and his deeds have written for the time in which he served, one of the most influential pages in the public life of Indiana.

ADOPTED by the Indianapolis Bar Association, the 12th day of February, 1958.

The Court now orders the above Resolution spread of record on the Order Books of this Court, and the Clerk of this Court is ordered to deliver a copy of said Resolution to the Reporter of this Court, who is ordered to print and publish the same in the Indiana Reports.

Dated February 21, 1958.

James A. Emmert
Chief Justice

(1)

Dan Collins Flanagan
⌒ 1899-1960 ⌒

- Born April 23, 1899, in Lafayette, Tippecanoe County, Indiana.

- Graduated from Frankfort (Indiana) High School.

- Served as a sergeant in World War I.

- Received a law degree from Benjamin Harrison Law School (now Indiana University School of Law—Indianapolis) in 1921.

- Served as deputy prosecutor for both the city of Fort Wayne and Allen County, Indiana.

- Served as county attorney for Allen County in 1940.

- Taught at both Valparaiso (Valparaiso, Indiana) University and the University of Notre Dame.

- Appointed to the Appellate Court of Indiana in 1941, serving there until 1949.

- Served on the Indiana Supreme Court from April 1, 1953, to December 31, 1954.

- Died February 28, 1960, in Fort Wayne, Allen County, Indiana.

IN MEMORIAM

DAN C. FLANAGAN

1899-1960

On February 28, 1960, at 10:00 o'clock in the morning the Creator saw fit to take from our midst a beloved and respected citizen of this community and a member of the Allen County Bar, Judge Dan C. Flanagan.

Dan was born on April 23, 1899, at Lafayette, Indiana, where his father Dan Patrick Flanagan practiced law, and it was inevitable that Dan should follow in his footsteps. He graduated from high school in Frankfort, Indiana and later enlisted in the Armed Services where he served with distinction as a Sergeant in the Field Artillery of World War I. After his separation from the Services, he enrolled in the Benjamin Harrison Law School, which is now known as the Indiana University School of Law, and graduated from this school with honors.

Immediately upon his graduation from law school he hung his shingle in Frankfort, Indiana, and practiced law there until 1924 when he moved to Fort Wayne.

Upon moving to Fort Wayne, he first became associated with the law firm of Heaton & Heaton. In the year 1931 he became a member of the firm of Leonard, Rose, Flanagan and McCreevy.

In 1925, shortly after coming to Fort Wayne, he became acquainted with Mabelle Cass, and Dan and Mabelle were married on October 5, 1925; and to this union one son, Daniel C. Flanagan, Jr., was born.

(xli)

In 1934 the firm of Flanagan and Murphy was established and Dan was associated with Jim Murphy until 1937 when he became associated with Charles Bond in the firm then known as Flanagan and Bond.

Probably few members of this Association shall ever enjoy such a varied and interesting career, such as was Dan's good fortune to enjoy. He not only held the top political offices of his party in this county but also the highest office of his profession in this state. He served as Deputy Prosecutor in Clinton County in 1921 and 1922 and as Deputy Prosecutor in Allen County in 1929 and 1930. In 1936 Dan became Chairman of the Allen County Republican Central Committee and it was immediately after his assumption of the chairmanship of that committee that the fortunes of the Republican Party changed for the better, and during Dan's term as County Chairman many successful campaigns were conducted.

January 1, 1940 Dan was named Allen County Attorney and served in this capacity for approximately one year, at which time he was appointed to the Appellate Court by the Governor of the State of Indiana, for which office he later was a candidate, being the only candidate in history to win a State Convention nomination by acclamation four consecutive times. He won the office in 1940 and 1944 and served in this capacity until 1948, at which time he returned to the general practice of law until again called to public service by the Governor when a vacancy occurred on the Supreme Court bench. Dan was appointed as a member of the Supreme Court of the State of Indiana in 1953 and served in that capacity until January of 1955. During this time as a member of the Appellate and Supreme Court Judge Flanagan handed down many profound and sound opinions, which are still being followed by the upper courts.

Dan returned to the practice of law again in Fort
Wayne and in May of 1959 formed a new law firm with
Robert S. McCain, which law firm was in existence at
the time of Dan's death.

Dan, during his lifetime, was the recipient of many
honors, having been named at one time to the Valparaiso
University Law College extension lecture staff and also
served on the permanent lecture staff of the University
of Notre Dame. Of course everyone in the legal profession is acquainted with the fact that Dan was the
author of several textbooks which have gained wide
reputation and use throughout the profession, and, as
a matter of fact, have been cited numerous times by
the upper courts in their decisions.

In addition to the heavy load that Dan carried as a
lawyer, judge, and author of legal textbooks, he always
found time to be active in the Allen County Bar Association, Indiana State Bar Association, and American
Bar Association, of which he was a member; and was
always a willing and eager worker in civic and religious
endeavor, being a member of St. Patrick's Church, Holy
Name Society, Fourth Degree Knights of Columbus,
and President of the Ancient Order of Hibernians.

During his lifetime he was never too busy to help
and assist a young lawyer, and was always available
to give advice or assistance whenever he could. During
the latter part of his practice Dan often served in a
consulting capacity for other lawyers and his keen
insight into the law and his ability to immediately grasp
the problems involved in any type of a lawsuit made
him a most worthy opponent. It was not only a joy
to work with Dan, it was also a pleasure to try a lawsuit against him because from the beginning it was
always a battle of wits. When Dan appeared in court,
the court was always well pleased to see him representing a client inasmuch as he knew that his client would

have skilled representation, and that the legal points involved would remain clear-cut.

It is by no means intended that these few brief remarks should be a complete summation of Dan's illustrious career and life. The presentation of merely the highlights alone would consume hours of time. If ever there existed a person who understood the value, use, meaning and purpose of life, it was Dan Flanagan.

Dan was a considerate husband and devoted father, and his passing was untimely. All of us know that Dan did not regard his life's work as complete. Had he lived, the balance of his life would have been devoted to service of his fellow man. We all feel a great sense of personal loss at his passing. We shall miss him.

Therefore, Be It Resolved that the Allen County Indiana Bar Association give a public expression of the sorrow of its members on the death of Judge Dan C. Flanagan.

Be It Further Resolved that a copy of this Resolution be transmitted to the widow and son of Judge Flanagan.

Be It Further Resolved that this Resolution be placed of record in the permanent records of the Courts of Allen County, Indiana.

> Respectfully submitted,
> Allen County Bar Association
> by Memorial Resolutions Committee

William H. Schannen, Judge
Allen Circuit Court
Harold E. Korn, Judge
Allen Superior Court No. 2
C. Byron Hayes

Lloyd S. Hartzler, Judge
Allen Superior Court No. 3
William L. Burger, Judge
Superior Court of Allen County
L. H. Dunten

ORDER

The court orders the above Resolution spread of record on the Order Books of this court, and the Clerk of this court is ordered to deliver a copy of said Resolution to the Reporter of this court, who is ordered to print and publish the same in the Indiana Reports.

Done at Indianapolis, Indiana, this the 19th day of May, 1961.

Arch N. Bobbitt, Chief Justice

Oliver Starr

⸻ 1883-1961 ⸻

- Born December 10, 1883, in Wells County, Indiana.

- Obtained a bachelor's degree from Indiana University in 1905.

- Received a law degree from the University of Michigan in 1908.

- Admitted to practice law in Indiana in 1908.

- Held the posts of city attorney in Gary, Lake County, Indiana, and prosecuting attorney for Lake County, Indiana.

- Practiced law in Gary for many years.

- Served on the Indiana Supreme Court from January 1, 1945, to January 1, 1951.

- Died March 1961, in Chesterton, Porter County, Indiana.

IN MEMORIAM

OLIVER STARR

1883-1961

WHEREAS, Oliver Starr was a native Hoosier, having been born in 1883 on a farm near Bluffton, in Wells County; schooled in the common schools of his home State; and having received his advanced education at Indiana University, where he received his AB degree and at the University of Michigan where he received his LLB degree, having been graduated from each of these great institutions of higher learning with highest honors; and

WHEREAS, after teaching school in Indiana in his early years, Judge Starr later engaged in the practice of his chosen profession in the city of Gary, in Lake County, where he achieved a well deserved reputation as one of the great advocates of his time; and

WHEREAS, as a lifelong Republican, Judge Starr became well known for his public service, having served as the county chairman of his party, and having further served with distinction as city attorney of the city of Gary; as Prosecuting Attorney of Lake County; and having been at one time his party's candidate for Judge of the Appellate Court of Indiana, and for Representative in the Congress of the United States from the First District of Indiana; and

WHEREAS, in 1944 he was elected to serve as a Judge of the Supreme Court of Indiana, and served in that capacity for six years, beginning in 1945 and ending in 1950, not thereafter seeking re-election; and

(xlvi)

WHEREAS, Judge Starr had a profound knowledge of the law and an inflexible determination to administer it without fear or favor; and

WHEREAS, the decisions he wrote as a Judge of our highest Court will, to his honor and credit, live long as a guiding light to Judges and lawyers who have followed and who will follow after him; and

WHEREAS, he was the proud and affectionate father of three sons and two daughters, and was universally known and respected as a father, a friend, a lawyer and a jurist of whom the members of his professions are justly proud, and whose passing is mourned by all who knew him.

BE IT, THEREFORE, RESOLVED: that we of the Gary Bar Association go on record as expressing our respect and admiration for him, our absent member, and that we extend our deepest sympathy to his family and loved ones.

Dated at Gary, Indiana, this 10th day of May, 1961.

Respectfully submitted,
GARY BAR ASSOCIATION
By Floyd S. Draper
Frank V. Roman
William I. Marlatt

ORDER

The court orders the foregoing Resolution spread of record on the Order Books of this court, and the Clerk of this court is ordered to deliver a copy of said Resolution to the Reporter of this court, who is ordered to print and publish the same in the Indiana Reports.

Dated at Indianapolis, Indiana, this 19th day of May, 1961.

Arch N. Bobbitt, Chief Justice

Julius Curtis Travis

⌒ 1868-1961 ⌒

- Born July 31, 1868, in LaPorte County, Indiana.

- Received a bachelor's degree from the University of Michigan and then a law degree in 1894.

- Managed the University of Michigan varsity football and baseball teams for three years.

- Worked as a sports editor for several newspapers, including the *Chicago Tribune*.

- Served as a prosecutor for several years.

- Served two terms on the Indiana Supreme Court, from January 3, 1921, until January 1, 1933.

- Served on the Selective Service Appeals Board during both World War I and World War II.

- Died March 11, 1961, in Indianapolis, Marion County, Indiana.

IN MEMORIAM

JULIUS C. TRAVIS

1868-1961

Judge Julius C. Travis, born July 31, 1868, in LaPorte County, Indiana, died in Indianapolis on March 11, 1961.

Impaired health during youth kept him from high school graduation until 1888 following which he entered the University of Michigan. Here he suffered the loss of eyesight requiring a reader for his studies, then surgery to restore his vision. Family and friends encouraged him after three years to re-enter college to pursue his professional law studies.

His keen mind and determination to catch up led him into a variety of campus leadership activities, including: co-organizer and business manager of the Michigan Daily and the Inlander (campus publications); manager for three years of the varsity football and baseball teams; correspondent sports editor for the Chicago Tribune, Detroit News, Cleveland Plain Dealer, Philadelphia Ledger and Boston Transcript; a founder and secretary of the American Republican League under the supervision of the then Major William McKinley and General Benjamin Harrison. He represented that League at conventions in Louisville, Kentucky, and Syracuse, New York. During his senior year he joined the Kappa Sigma fraternity.

Upon graduation he read and took up the practice of law at LaPorte, Indiana, but supplemented his income by selling insurance. In 1896 he married Ethel Closser. They had four children: Dr. Richard C. Travis (de-

(xlviii)

ceased), Mrs. Elizabeth McGowan, Howard P. Travis (attorney at Indianapolis) and Dr. Julius C. Travis, Jr. The Judge and Mrs. Travis together enjoyed a well-earned happiness of marriage for 65 years.

In business at LaPorte, while engaging in building a successful law practice, he organized and operated the Rustic Hickory Furniture Mfg. Co. and the LaPorte Lumber & Coal Co., the latter being now family operated. His Marshfield Farms were devoted to the raising of pure bred livestock and in cultivating fine grains and fruit. His prize cattle and sheep won Blue Ribbons at the Chicago Livestock Shows. At 18 he became an active trader in the grain market and continued his investment trading in such commodities until 1960.

In public life, he was city and county attorney, prosecutor, judge and a member of the Selective Service Appeal Board in World Wars I and II. In 1920 he was elected Judge of the Indiana Supreme Court, then in 1926 was re-elected for an additional six-year term. He was a renowned lecturer on the Constitutional Law of the United States and on the Law and Literature of our times. In every situation his forthright and intellectual honesty in dealing with involved and controversial matters was never questioned. Even at 90 years he was rugged in mind and spirit as he was in body. He continued in the practice of law at Indianapolis after retirement from the Supreme Court, his chief interests being to read and study in the fields of history, law, classical literature, biographies and the writings of Emanuel Swedenborg. He held memberships in the Alumni Advisory Council and Lawyers Club at the University of Michigan, in the Indiana and American Bar Associations, the American Law Institute and was a Swedenborgian.

He was an active alumnus of his Kappa Sigma fraternity, having served as its National president. He contributed much to aid and assist undergraduate students that they might be better prepared to enjoy successful living and to encourage them to become worthy citizens to maintain a sound and free government.

The world is a better place because Judge Julius C. Travis has lived among us.

ORDER

The foregoing memorial to the late Julius C. Travis having this day been adopted by the Supreme Court of Indiana;

IT IS HEREBY ORDERED by the court that such memorial be published in the official reports of the Supreme Court of Indiana.

Dated at Indianapolis, Indiana, this the ninth day of May, 1961.

Arch N. Bobbitt, Chief Justice
Indiana Supreme Court

James Peter Hughes
⎯ 1874-1961 ⎯

- Born December 18, 1874, near Terre Haute, Vigo County, Indiana.

- Received a bachelor of philosophy degree from DePauw University (Greencastle, Indiana) in 1898 and a law degree from Indiana University in 1900.

- Admitted to the Indiana bar in 1900.

- Practiced law in Greencastle, Putnam County, Indiana.

- Served as a prosecutor from 1902 to 1911 and a circuit judge from 1911 to 1933.

- Served on the Indiana Supreme Court from January 3, 1933, to January 1, 1936.

- Practiced law from 1941 until his retirement.

- Died August 30, 1961, in Greencastle, Putnam County, Indiana.

In Memoriam

Judge James Peter Hughes was an able lawyer and a highly respected jurist. He began the practice of law in the city of Greencastle, Indiana, in the year 1900, and since that time and until his death, August 30, 1961, he was in some way connected with the legal profession. He was at the time of his death the oldest and best known member of the Putnam County Bar.

He was born December 18, 1874, in Vigo County, Indiana, and his forbears were sturdy pioneers of Irish lineage. His father was George W. Hughes and his mother was Hessie Ferrel Hughes. At an early age the family moved to a farm near Cloverdale, Indiana.

Judge Hughes attended the county schools, DePauw Preparatory school and was graduated from DePauw University in 1898. After graduation he entered Indiana Law School at Indianapolis, Indiana, from which he was graduated in 1900.

After his graduation he began the practice of law in Greencastle, Indiana. He was the junior member of the firm of Allee and Hughes. He was County Attorney, Deputy Prosecuting Attorney and was elected Prosecuting Attorney for the old 13th Judicial Circuit, composed of Putnam and Clay Counties, in 1911. While serving as Prosecuting Attorney the 64th Judicial Circuit was created, to be known as the Putnam Circuit Court of Putnam County, Indiana, and Governor Thomas R. Marshall then appointed him as Judge of the newly created circuit. He was re-elected four times, continuing to serve as Circuit Judge until the year 1933 when he was elected to the Indiana Supreme

(xl)

Court. He was a Judge in the Indiana Supreme Court for six years, and then returned to Greencastle and resumed the practice of law in partnership with his son, James G. Hughes, which association has continued until the time of his death.

He was a member of the Methodist Church, Masonic Lodge and Delta Upsilon Fraternity, and took an active interest in Democratic politics.

Judge Hughes was first married to Mary Ellen Gainer Hughes who died in 1932. He is survived by his widow, Margaret Conlin Hughes, his son, James G. Hughes, and two grandchildren, Lieutenant James E. Hughes and Jane Ellen Hughes.

He was an able trial judge. His written opinions when a member of the Indiana Supreme Court were based upon careful study, clear legal reasoning and sound judgment.

As a lawyer at the bar he discharged his duties honestly, faithfully and successfully. His life was the law. He was an able, vigorous and successful advocate, a wise and honest counselor, an honest and just judge.

ADOPTED by the Putnam County Bar Association.

Frank G. Stoessel
John H. Allee
Francis N. Hamilton

IN THE
SUPREME COURT OF INDIANA
RE: ADOPTION OF MEMORIAL TO
THE LATE JAMES PETER HUGHES

ORDER

The Court orders the foregoing Resolution spread of record on the Order Books of this Court, and the Clerk of this Court is ordered to deliver a copy of said Resolution to the Reporter of this Court, who is ordered to print and publish the same in the Indiana Reports.

(xli)

Dated at Indianapolis, Indiana, this 15th day of November, 1961.

S/Frederick Landis

_____

Frederick Landis,
Chief Justice

Howard Sloan Young, Sr.

1879-1961

- Born August 7, 1879, in Indianapolis, Marion County, Indiana.

- Graduated from the University of Chicago in 1898.

- Received a law degree from the Indiana Law School in 1903.

- Admitted to the Indiana bar in 1903.

- Served as United States Commissioner from 1920 to 1944.

- Practiced law from 1904 to 1944.

- Served as president of the Indianapolis Bar Association from 1931 to 1932.

- Served as a member of the Indianapolis School Board.

- Elected to the Indiana Supreme Court in 1944, serving from January 1, 1945, to January 1, 1951.

- Returned to private practice of law with his son, Howard S. Young, Jr. in 1951.

- Died October 14, 1961, in Indianapolis, Marion County, Indiana.

In Memoriam

Howard S. Young was born in 1879 in Indianapolis, Marion County, Indiana, where he was a lifetime resident. He died at his home, 7575 North Illinois Street, on October 14, 1961.

He graduated from the University of Chicago in 1898 and completed his legal education at the Indiana Law School in 1903. Except for his service as Judge of the Indiana Supreme Court (1945-1951), he engaged in the active practice of law after his admission until his death. In 1931-1932, he was President of the Indianapolis Bar Association. He was United States Commissioner from 1920 to 1944. He was selected as a member of the Indianapolis School Board from which he resigned upon election to the Supreme Court. Prior to that election he was a member of the law firm of Fessler, Elam & Young. Following his retirement from the Supreme Court he was associated with his son, Howard S. Young, Jr. in the firm of Young & Young.

Judge Young was always active in the civic and political life of the community and faithful as a member of the state and local Bar Associations. He was always fair in his dealings with his fellow lawyers and firm in his convictions in matters handled for clients. His thoroughness in preparation to the best of his ability gained for him a reputation of being an excellent advocate. His decisions were well reasoned, carefully and concisely expressed in accordance with rules of procedure and the law applicable.

(xliii)

Judge Young was survived by his son, Howard S. Young, Jr., his daughter, Mrs. Frederick G. Johns of Arcadia, California, a brother, Byron C. Young of Lafayette, Indiana, and thirteen grandchildren. It is with deep regret that we, among his many friends and acquaintances, mark his passing.

ADOPTED by the Indianapolis Bar Association.

MEMORIAL COMMITTEE
Harvey Grabill
Emsley Johnson
Paul R. Summers
Frank Symmes, Sr.
Harry E. Yockey, Chairman

IN THE
SUPREME COURT OF INDIANA
RE: ADOPTION OF MEMORIAL TO
THE LATE HOWARD S. YOUNG

ORDER

The Court orders the foregoing Resolution spread of record on the Order Books of this Court, and the Clerk of this Court is ordered to deliver a copy of said Resolution to the Reporter of this Court, who is ordered to print and publish the same in the Indiana Reports.

Dated at Indianapolis, Indiana, this 16th day of November, 1961.

S/Frederick Landis

Frederick Landis,
Chief Justice

Harold Edward Achor

~ 1908-1967 ~

- Born November 16, 1907, in Coffeeville, Kansas.

- Completed public school in Atwood, Kosciusko County, Indiana.

- Graduated from Indiana Central College (now University of Indianapolis), Indianapolis, Indiana, in 1928.

- Earned a law degree from Indiana University in 1931.

- Practiced law, as a member of the firm Achor & Peck in Anderson, Madison County, Indiana, from 1931 to 1942.

- Taught speech and political science at Anderson College (Anderson, Indiana) from 1932 to 1937.

- Elected Madison Superior Court Judge in 1942.

- Elected to the Indiana Appellate Court for a four-year term in 1950.

- Left his Indiana appellate court seat to serve on the Indiana Supreme Court in 1955.

Continued ~

Harold Edward Achor

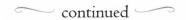 continued

- Resigned from the Indiana Supreme Court in 1966 due to poor health.

- Served as a member of the Board of Governors of the Associated Colleges of Indiana.

- Served on the Board of Trustees of Anderson College.

- Died February 5, 1967, in Anderson, Madison County, Indiana.

IN THE

SUPREME COURT

OF INDIANA

NOVEMBER TERM, 1966

ORDER OF ADJOURNMENT

IN MEMORIAM OF

HAROLD E. ACHOR, ASSOCIATE JUDGE

WHEREAS, this Court has learned with shock and sorrow of the regrettable death of our former Associate and respected member of this Court, Harold E. Achor, and

WHEREAS, he has been a learned teacher, an able lawyer, and an exemplary Judge in Madison County Superior Court, and in the Appellate Court and the Supreme Court of Indiana, and

WHEREAS, the State of Indiana has lost an illustrious citizen and good friend who was dedicated to the search for truth and justice, and who gave willingly of himself in advancing many civic causes, and

WHEREAS, his presence and assistance will be missed by his colleagues and the Citizens of Indiana for many years,

IT IS THEREFORE RESOLVED AND ORDERED that the Supreme Court of Indiana stand adjourned in memoriam of Harold E. Achor until 10:00 A. M., Wednesday, February 8th, 1967, and the Clerk of this

xlv

Court is directed to spread this order in memoriam on the records of this Court and transmit a copy hereof to his bereaved wife and daughters, all of which is done this 7th day of February, 1967.

(s)   Norman F. Arterburn
Chief Justice

Witness the seal of this Court,
this 7th day of February, 1967.

In Memoriam

To: The Chief Judge and Members of the Appellate Court of Indiana

Your Committee reports the following memorial of Judge Harold E. Achor, who, at the time of his death, on February 5, 1967, was a resident of Anderson, Indiana.

Harold E. Achor was born 59 years ago in Coffeyville, Kansas, and as an infant he was brought by his parents to Kosciusko County, Indiana, where he attended schools at Atwood and thereafter attended and graduated from Indiana Central College. He graduated from Indiana University School of Law in 1931, and returned to Anderson, where he engaged in the practice of law until 1942, the year in which he was elected Judge of the Madison Superior Court, serving two terms on that Court.

In 1950 Judge Achor was elected to the Indiana Appellate Court for a four year term, following which he served two six year terms as a member of the Supreme Court of Indiana, resigning from that Court in December, 1966, because of ill health.

Judge Achor was a high minded citizen, a teacher at Anderson College during the period of his general practice of law at Anderson, an outstanding lawyer, and a conscientious and upright Judge. He was courteous and deferential in his treatment of the members of this Court and of the lawyers who appeared before him. His opinions revealed an analytical mind and a determination to see that justice always prevailed.

While teaching at Anderson College Judge Achor married Miss Helen Martin, daughter of Dr. Earl L. Martin, Vice President of the college. He is survived by his wife and their two daughters, Mrs. Dianne Spell and Mrs. Lana Dean, and one grandson.

Russell W. Smith, Judge
Charles W. Cook, Judge
Committee on Resolutions

This memorial having been reported to the full Court is by the Court approved and adopted as the memorial of this Court and ordered spread of record upon the permanent records of this Court. Ordered published in the official reports of this Court.

Respectfully submitted,

James C. Cooper, Chief Justice
Joseph O. Carson, Judge
Thomas J. Faulconer, Judge
George H. Prime, Judge
John W. Pfaff, Presiding Judge
G. Remy Bierly, Judge
Russell W. Smith, Judge
Charles W. Cook, Judge

February 20, 1967

RESOLUTION

OF THE

INDIANA STATE BAR ASSOCIATION

IN MEMORY OF

THE HONORABLE HAROLD E. ACHOR

JUDGE OF THE SUPREME COURT OF

INDIANA

On behalf of the Indiana State Bar Association, its Board of Managers notes with deep regret the passing of former Indiana Supreme Court Judge Harold E. Achor on February 5, 1967. Upon motion duly made, seconded and unanimously carried, the following resolution is adopted for inclusion in the minutes of this meeting and the Secretary is directed to deliver a copy thereof to Judge Achor's family.

WHEREAS, the late Harold E. Achor was a jurist of extraordinary legal talent and a man of many accomplishments, and,

WHEREAS, he served Madison County well as Judge of the Superior Court of that County for two terms, and,

WHEREAS, he served the entire State of Indiana with distinction first during one term on the Indiana Appellate Court, and, thereafter, during two terms on the Indiana Supreme Court, and,

WHEREAS, he worked closely with this Association in the processing of grievances through the Disciplinary Commission of the Indiana Supreme Court, and,

WHEREAS, he was an active and interested worker in his church, the Park Place Church of God in Anderson, Indiana, and,

WHEREAS, he devoted much time to the furtherance and development of that denomination's Theological Seminary, serving for many, many years as a member of the Board of Trustees of Anderson College,

NOW, THEREFORE, BE IT RESOLVED that the regret and profound sorrow of the Indiana State Bar Association upon the occasion of the death of Judge Achor, and the feeling of admiration of its membership for his distinguished career as a legal scholar and jurist of eminence be spread of record on the annals of this Association, and a copy hereof sent to his family.

(s) Mentor Kraus
President, Indiana State Bar Association

Attest:
(s) Robert Morgan
Secretary, Indiana State Bar Association

1

RESOLUTION

OF THE

MADISON COUNTY BAR ASSOCIATION

IN MEMORY OF

THE HONORABLE HAROLD E. ACHOR, DE-

CEASED,

FEBRUARY 5, 1967.

The members of the Madison County Bar Association are profoundly shocked and grieved by the death
on February 5, 1967, of one of its most distinguished
members, the Honorable Harold E. Achor, retired Justice of the Indiana Supreme Court.

Harold E. Achor started his practice of law in Anderson, Indiana in 1932 and continued in private practice until he was elected Judge of the Superior Court of
Madison County in 1942. He was re-elected to this office in 1946. In 1950 he was elected to serve a four
year term on the Appellate Court of the State of Indiana. In 1954 he was elected to the Supreme Court of
the State of Indiana for a six year term and was
re-elected in 1960 for another such term. He served
as Chief Justice of the Indiana Supreme Court many
times. He retired in December of 1966 because of illness.

Judge Achor in his ten years of practice in Madison
County, was sincere, honest, aggressive and resourceful and was a well respected and able lawyer. He
served as a Judge of the Superior Court of Madison

li

County, the Appellate Court and the Supreme Court of the State of Indiana with great honor, credit and distinction to the legal profession, the Bar associations and the Judiciary of the State of Indiana. He advanced further in the State Judiciary of Indiana than any other lawyer from Madison County prior to his time. His sincere and well founded opinions in the Appellate and Supreme Courts of the State of Indiana will stand forever as a monument to his integrity, skill, ability and fair dealing.

Judge Achor was always a kind, gracious, patient and friendly person, interested in other people. He was a constant churchman and participated in many civic activities and served on the Board of Trustees of Anderson College for some 20 years. He was a fine family man, husband and father and leaves a widow, Helen E. Achor, and two daughters and a grandson and a great host of friends to mourn his loss.

The Madison County Bar Association mourns the loss of one of its most distinguished members and extends to the widow and family its heartfelt sympathy.

NOW, THEREFORE, BE IT HEREBY RESOLVED by the Madison County Bar Association in special memorial session this 8th day of February, 1967, that this resolution be adopted as a memoriam to the Honorable Harold E. Achor, deceased, and spread of record in the order books of the Circuit and Superior Courts of Madison County, Indiana, and a copy delivered to the widow and family.

On motion and second of this resolution, it was unanimously passed by the members of the Madison

County Bar Association, assembled in memorial session this 8th day of February, 1967.

MADISON COUNTY BAR ASSOCIATION,
By:

/s/   Robert W. Miller
      President

/s/   William R. Clifford
      Secretary

RESOLUTIONS COMMITTEE,
By:

/s/   Harold J. Anderson
      Harold Anderson

      William Byer

/s/   William L. Peck
      William L. Peck

Walter Myers, Jr.

⟶ 1914- 1967 ⟵

- Born June 9, 1914, in Indianapolis, Marion County, Indiana.

- Graduated from Yale University in 1935.

- Received a law degree from Yale Law School in 1938.

- Opened a legal practice in Indianapolis in 1939.

- Lectured in business law at Butler University (Indianapolis, Indiana) beginning in 1943.

- Elected to the Indiana Appellate Court in 1958, serving until 1962.

- Elected to the Indiana Supreme Court, serving from January 7, 1963, until his death.

- Died June 2, 1967, in Indianapolis, Marion County, Indiana.

IN THE

SUPREME COURT

OF INDIANA

NOVEMBER TERM, 1966

ORDER OF ADJOURNMENT

IN MEMORIAM OF

WALTER MYERS, JR., ASSOCIATE JUDGE

WHEREAS, this Court has learned with shock and distress of the untimely death of one of our Associates, Walter Myers, Jr., a distinguished member of this Court, and

WHEREAS, he has enjoyed an outstanding career as a lawyer in Marion County and as a Judge of the Appellate Court and the Supreme Court of Indiana, and

WHEREAS, the citizens of the State of Indiana have lost an eminent jurist and one who was devoted to civic affairs and gave unstintingly of his service to laudable civic enterprises, his untimely loss will be felt by his fellow citizens of Indiana for many years to come,

NOW THEREFORE BE IT RESOLVED AND ORDERED that the Supreme Court of Indiana stand adjourned in memoriam of Walter Myers, Jr., our fellow Judge, until 2:00 P.M., Monday, June 5th, 1967, and the Clerk of this Court is directed to spread this order in memoriam on the records of this Court

lv

and transmit a copy hereof to his bereaved widow and sons, to his father, mother, brother and sister, all of which is done this 2nd day of June, 1967, at 1:00 P.M.

(s)   Donald H. Hunter
Chief Justice

Witness the seal of this Court,
this 2nd day of June, 1967.

In Memoriam

WALTER MYERS, JR.

We, the members of the Appellate Court of Indiana, adopt the following memorial on the life of Walter Myers, Jr., this 5th day of June, 1967:

Walter Myers, Jr. was born in Indianapolis, Indiana, on June 9, 1914, and died in Community Hospital in the city of Indianapolis on June 2, 1967, after an illness of six weeks.

He obtained his early education in the public schools of the city of Indianapolis and graduated from Yale University in 1935 and Yale Law School in 1938. Judge Myers was elected to the Appellate Court of Indiana for a four year term in 1958, and while still a member of the Appellate Court he was nominated and elected as one of the Judges of the Supreme Court, in 1962.

He was a person of fine character. He was a man of generous impulses and at all times he was courteous in his treatment of his colleagues, both as a practitioner and as a Judge. He was a lifelong member of the Democratic Party and supported its principles. He was a born lawyer from a family of lawyers, and was possessed of a keen legal mind.

He was an able, industrious and painstaking Judge. During his service as a member of the Appellate Court and the Supreme Court, he wrote many important opinions. He was careful and conscientious in the writing of his opinions and he spared no effort in arriving at a just determination.

Judge Myers was always interested and active in public and civic affairs in his home community and in the State.

He was a member of Pentalpha Masonic Lodge, Scottish Rite, Murat Shrine, and Tau Kappa Epsilon fraternity. He was an active member of the Second Presbyterian Church. He gave freely of his time to the Indianapolis, Indiana State, and American Bar Associations.

Judge Myers is survived by his widow, Jane; son, Dennis Myers and stepson, John R. Kinghan; his parents, Walter Myers and Katheryn Myers; his brother, Municipal Court Judge Joseph N. Myers, and his sister, Mrs. J. K. Northam.

We sincerely regret his passing, and we extend our sympathy to his bereaved family and friends. We feel keenly the loss of an outstanding lawyer and Judge.

This memorial is approved and adopted as the memorial of this Court and ordered spread of record upon the permanent records of this Court, and published in the official reports of this Court.

> John W. Pfaff, Chief Justice
> Joseph O. Carson, Presiding Judge
> James C. Cooper, Judge
> Charles W. Cook, Judge
> G. Remy Bierly, Judge
> George H. Prime, Judge
> Russell W. Smith, Judge
> Thomas J. Faulconer, Judge

TRIBUTE OF

INDIANA STATE BAR ASSOCIATION

TO THE MEMORY OF

HONORABLE WALTER MYERS, JR.,

JUDGE OF THE SUPREME COURT OF INDIANA

Walter Myers, Jr., died June 2, 1967.

The Indiana State Bar Association presents this tribute to him, a tribute of affection and a tender of the praise that is due him.

He was a lifetime resident of Indianapolis and one of a family of distinguished Indiana lawyers and public servants. His father, Walter Myers, Sr., is a pioneer Indianapolis lawyer, formerly Speaker of the Indiana General Assembly and, for thirteen years, Assistant Postmaster General of the United States. His brother, Joseph N. Myers, has served with high distinction for many years as Judge of the Municipal Court at Indianapolis. His brother-in-law, James K. Northam, was Deputy Attorney General of the State of Indiana and First Assistant Attorney General before he and Judge Myers became partners in the practice of law. All were graduated from Yale University, where Judge Myers received his AB in 1935 and his LL.B. in 1938.

Upon commencing the practice of law, Judge Myers entered into a lifelong service in the Democratic Party—as a precinct committeeman, then as a ward chairman, and later as nominee, first for Judge of the Superior Court of Marion County, then for Judge of the Marion Circuit Court.

He served also as Deputy Prosecuting Attorney and as attorney for the Board of Sanitary Commissioners.

lix

In 1958 he was nominated as a Democratic candidate for Judge of the Appellate Court of Indiana and was elected. After four years as an outstanding member of that court, in 1962 he was nominated and elected for a six-year term on the Supreme Court of Indiana.

But his service was by no means limited to his party and to the Bench and Bar. His was a very active life as a leader in the civic and charitable affairs of his community.

He was a past-president and long-time member of the Board of Managers of the YMCA Central Branch and also was a member of the Board and former President of the Marion County Tuberculosis Association. One of the activities closest to his heart was as a member of the board of Suemma Coleman Home and in positions dealing with the adoption of orphans. He was always interested in young people and for many years has been active as chairman of the Indianapolis Yale Club's committee which interviews applicants for admission to that university.

Beginning with 1943, and throughout the years until his death, he found time in his very active life to lecture in Business Law at Butler University.

November 26, 1952, he married Jane Weldon Kinghan. She brought to him great happiness and inspiration. His friends at once became her devoted friends. She lent her charm and energies to all his endeavors and was a true helpmeet.

With all his outside activities, Walter Myers was essentially a family man—devoted to his wife and two sons, to his father and mother and his brother and sister. Justifiably, he took great pride in his family.

He was a religious man, and he and his wife were active in the affairs of the Second Presbyterian Church.

Judge Myers was truly a friendly man. He genuinely liked people. He talked easily to any chance

acquaintance wherever he went. He formed devoted
friendships with many people in all walks of life. He
earned friendships by his own friendly treatment of
everyone he met. He kept these friendships green as he
climbed the ladder to the highest judicial office of his
state. He retained the devotion of his friends by remaining the same unassuming, outgoing kind of person
all his life.

Judge Myers served with distinction for more than
eight years as Judge upon the highest courts of his
state. He had a good legal mind and was industrious,
conscientious and energetic in the discharge of his
duties. He had an avid interest in all matters touching
upon the conduct of the courts and took a particular
interest in the problems of their administration. He
strove to improve the court wherever he could.

He was particularly mindful of the need for mod-
ernizing the courts of Indiana and devising ways to
improve the administration of the courts and the discharge of the increasingly heavy burdens cast upon
them.

As a judge, he was uniformly courteous and considerate to lawyers appearing before him and was
tolerant and sympathetic toward the problems of litigants before him.

With his fellow judges, he was kindly and generous.
Always cooperative and even tempered, he was helpful
in making the court the cohesive body so necessary to
its effective functioning.

Judge Myers' work on the Appellate and Supreme
Court is spread out for posterity in the bound volumes
of the Reports of those courts. His opinions will be
examined and studied by law students, professors, lawyers and judges. They will be cited, quoted, praised and
criticised for many generations to come.

His warm, friendly, attractive personality will live
on for many many years in the memories of his as-

sociates on this court and of the Bench and Bar of Indiana, all of whom have suffered a serious loss in his untimely death.

Respectfully submitted:

INDIANA STATE BAR ASSOCIATION
by
Mentor A. Kraus, President

Indianapolis, Indiana
June Fifth, 1967.

RESOLUTION

OF

THE INDIANAPOLIS BAR ASSOCIATION

WHEREAS, we have learned with shock and sorrow of the untimely death of our friend, Walter Myers, Jr., Judge of the Indiana Supreme Court, we of the Indianapolis Bar Association, who have been in the daily practice of the law with him, deem it appropriate to state our feeling of distress at the loss of a dear friend, to express the esteem in which we held him, and to extend to his widow and family our deepest sympathy.

Judge Myers, the lawyer, was a friend to all with whom he came in contact. We recall the professional associations we have had with him in the conduct of his clients' affairs; he was a counselor in whom his clients placed implicit confidence; he was an able advocate who asserted his cause with dignity and force; he was a lawyer who took pride in his professional skill, and in observing the ethics and courtesies of the profession. With it all, he acquired the friendship and deep respect of his brother lawyers. We remember the political campaigns in which he engaged with spirit and amiability, and attest that he enjoyed every day of his active life. As a true lawyer, he participated in the civic affairs of his community, and was an officer of his Church.

On the bench of both the Indiana Appellate and Supreme Courts, Judge Myers demonstrated keenness of intellect, a sound understanding of the law, and an ability of expression which has been of great assistance to us who are practitioners of the law. Although a proud member of his political party, he was nonpartisan in the exercise of his judicial duties. He was truly a distinguished member of a family distinguished in the law.

NOW, THEREFORE, Be it Resolved by the Indianapolis Bar Association that

We feel a great personal loss, and a loss to the legal profession and the Judiciary of the State of Indiana, in the untimely death of Walter Myers, Jr., Judge of the Indiana Supreme Court,

We send our deepest sympathy to his widow Jane, and to the other members of his family. They may take pride in the certain knowledge that he has made a significant contribution in his lifetime by his able service to his friends, his profession, and his State.

Donald Roosevelt Mote
⌒ 1900-1968 ⌒

- Born April 27, 1900, in Randolph County, Indiana.

- Attended DePauw University (Greencastle, Indiana), but graduated with a bachelor's degree from Wabash College (Crawfordsville, Indiana) in 1923.

- Received a law degree from George Washington University Law School in 1927.

- Worked for Secretary of Commerce Herbert Hoover and the United States Department of Justice during his time in Washington, D.C.

- Practiced law for thirty-five years in Indiana, first in Indianapolis and then in Wabash County.

- Served as Indiana Deputy Attorney General in 1928.

- Served as Wabash County attorney from 1957 to 1962.

- Served on the Indiana Appellate Court from 1962 to 1966.

- Elected to the Indiana Supreme Court in 1966, serving from January 3, 1967, until his death.

- Died September 17, 1968, in Indianapolis, Marion County, Indiana.

In Memoriam

CLERK OF THE SUPREME AND APPELLATE COURTS

The following resolution was adopted as a memorial to the Honorable Donald R. Mote:

Whereas, this Court has learned with shock and distress of the untimely death of one of our Associates, Donald R. Mote, a distinguished member of this Court, and,

Whereas, he has enjoyed an outstanding career as a lawyer in Marion and Wabash Counties and as a Judge of the Appellate Court and the Supreme Court of Indiana, and,

Whereas, the citizens of the State of Indiana have lost an eminent jurist and one who was devoted to civic affairs and gave unstintingly of his service to laudable civic enterprises, his untimely loss will be felt by his fellow citizens of Indiana for many years to come,

Now therefore be it resolved and ordered that the Supreme Court of Indiana stand adjourned in memoriam of Donald R. Mote, our fellow Judge, until 9:00 A.M., Monday, September 23, 1968, and the Clerk of this Court is directed to spread this order in memoriam on the records of this Court and transmit a copy hereof to his bereaved widow, daughter, son, granddaughters and sisters, all of which is done this 18th day of September, 1968 at 4:00 P.M.

/s/   Donald H. Hunter
Acting Chief Justice

Witness the seal of this Court, this 18th day of September, 1968.

xxxvii

In Memoriam

Donald R. Mote was born on a farm in Randolph County, Indiana, on April 27, 1900. He died on the 17th day of September, 1968, at Wabash, Indiana. He was married to Flora Hunter, and left surviving him his widow, his daughter, Mrs. Richard A. Walsman of Normal, Illinois; his son, Thomas N. Mote of Columbus; three sisters, Mrs. J. O. Miller of Maryville, Missouri, Mrs. Howard Harley of Indianapolis and Mrs. Oscar Spahr of Portland, and six granddaughters.

He attended DePauw University, and graduated from Wabash College where he received a bachelor of arts degree. He attended George Washingeon University School of Law at Washington, D.C., where he earned a bachelor of laws degree, and afterwards worked for the United States Secretary of Commerce, who at the time was Herbert C. Hoover, and also was associated with the Office of the United States Department of Justice. He practiced law in the City of Indianapolis for ten years and then moved to North Manchester in Wabash County in 1937. He maintained an office there until moving to his office and home in Wabash in 1958.

He was elected as Judge of the Appellate Court of the State of Indiana, in 1962, and served until January 1, 1967. In 1966, he was elected as a member of the Supreme Court of Indiana from the Fifth Judicial District. Both in Indianapolis and in Wabash County he was active in Republican politics. He served in Indianapolis as a Republican precinct committeeman and was employed as a deputy to former Indiana Attorney General Arthur Gilliam.

He was a former President of the Wabash County Bar Association, a member of the Indiana Judges' Association, the

RULES OF THE SUPREME COURT.   xxxix

Indiana State Bar Association and Phi Delta Phi legal fraternity. He was a former President of the North Manchester Kiwanis Club, a past member of the Board of Directors of the Little Red Door in Indianapolis, and a Member and Trustee of the Wabash Presbyterian Church.

He was active in fraternal organizations, having been a member of the North Manchester Masonic Lodge, the Fort Wayne Valley of the Scottish Rite, the Mizpah Shrine at Fort Wayne, Delta Tau Delta social fraternity, the Indiana Society of Chicago, the Wabash Elks Club, the Wabash Historical Society and the Wabash Rotary Club.

As a member of the Appellate Court of Indiana, he proved himself well qualified for the position. He was diligent in his work, aggressive in the presentation of his views, and his opinions were logical and well-written. At all times he sought to reach a right result, and by doing so, he won and held the confidence and respect of his fellow members of the Bench.

He was an able lawyer, an impartial judge, and, at all times had a high sense of civic duty and responsibility. We regret his passing.

/s/   John W. Pfaff,
       Judge

/s/   G. Remy Bierly,
       Judge

/s/   Russell W. Smith,
       Judge

IN THE

SUPREME COURT OF INDIANA

ORDER

The within and attached resolutions of the Wabash Circuit Court of Indiana in memoriam of Donald R. Mote are now by this Court ordered spread upon the record books of this Court.

The Clerk of this Court is hereby and herewith instructed to transmit copies hereof to Mrs. Donald R. Mote (Flora H.), his widow, at 60 West Hill St., Wabash, Indiana; Mrs. Richard L. Walsman (Virginia M.), his daughter, at 1100 Belt Ave., Normal, Illinois 61761; and Mr. Thomas N. Mote, his son, at 2514 Franklin Street, Columbus, Indiana 47201.

Done at Indianapolis, Indiana, this 21st day of October, 1968.

DAVID M. LEWIS, CHIEF JUSTICE

RESOLUTION OF THE
WABASH COUNTY BAR ASSOCIATION
ON THE DEATH OF
THE HONORABLE DONALD R. MOTE

In the passing of our good friend and colleague, The Honorable Donald R. Mote, the Wabash County Bar Association has suffered a great loss. Desiring to express our sympathy to his family, our respect and esteem for him and our deep sense of personal loss, we have, acting as a unit, adopted the following expression of our thoughts and feelings on the occasion of his death.

Judge Mote had a full life and an interesting and productive career. He was born in Randolph County and received his early education there. He attended DePauw University and was later graduated from Wabash College with an A.B. degree. His legal training was obtained at the Law School of George Washington University in Washington, D. C., from which he was graduated with an LL.B. degree. While attending law school, he worked in the Department of Commerce under the then Secretary of Commerce, the Honorable Herbert H. Hoover. He also served with the Department of Justice while in Washington. After his graduation he practiced law in Indianapolis with the firm of which former Appellate Judge Milton B. Hottel was the senior member. He also served as Deputy Attorney General under the late Arthur Gilliom. In 1937 he came to Wabash County, locating in North Manchester, where he practiced law for some years. Later he moved to Wabash and opened an office with the late Merl M. Wall. Later he was associated in the practice with Robert F. Gonderman and William H. Tallman. He was elected to the Appellate Court in 1962 and in 1966 was elected to the Supreme Court, of which court he was a member at the time of his death. His affiliations were many and varied and he gave of himself and his energies to many worthwhile activities.

An outstanding facet of his character was his complete devotion to his family, which consisted of his wife, Flora, a

xlii   RULES OF THE SUPREME COURT.

son and daughter and six grandchildren. In his busy life, he always gave precedence to them and their welfare and he frequently acknowledged the assistance and encouragement Mrs. Mote had given him throughout their marriage.

Judge Mote had, we think, the ideal temperament for a judge of a court of review. He was conscientious in this discharge of his duties, researched the cases carefully that he was called upon to decide, giving due consideration to the basic concepts of law as well as the established precedents, at the same time being ever mindful of the equities. He was thus able to achieve a balance between the technicalities which might be involved and the simple questions of fairness and justice to the interested parties. He was a person of strong convictions and always fought vigorously for the principles in which he believed even though the position he took was at the time an unpopular one. This was evidenced by the dissenting opinions he wrote. Certainly it could never be said that he was motivated to follow a course of action because it was expedient.

Don was deeply religious and contributed much to the Presbyterian Church in Wabash, of which he was a member and where he had served as a Trustee. He was, however, practical in the application of his religious beliefs and applied the spiritual values which he held dear to his daily life.

In politics, as everyone knows who had any contact with him, he was extremely partisan, but he was also fair and was quick to recognize good qualities in those in public office with whom he differed, and to concede, perhaps grudgingly, that his own party just might now and then have its weaknesses.

Perhaps Don's outstanding quality was his loyalty to his friends. He was always ready to lend assistance to a friend, but his code demanded loyalty in return. Did you fail to measure up to the standard he set for himself, there was no question of retaliation but the friendship simply ended.

Throughout the years of Judge Mote's practice in Wabash County, he was recognized as a formidable opponent. He prepared his cases well, presenting them with an earnestness and zeal for the protection of the rights of his clients that was notable. Indeed he served in the finest tradition of the legal profession.

Don was the only local lawyer to be elected to both the Appellate and Supreme Courts of the State. His record of service in those capacities has brought honor and distinction to the Wabash County Bar Association and we shall always be proud of his accomplishments as an Appellate and Supreme Court Justice.

To have been stricken at the height of his career, when he had so much to live for and to contribute, is indeed a tragedy, but the will to live and the courage he demonstrated will long be an inspiration to all of us.

To the family of Judge Mote, we extend our deepest sympathy. We hope they may find consolation in the memory of his distinguished career. Our sympathy goes, too, to the members of the Supreme Court, where we know he will be missed by his colleagues, and of the Appellate Court, where he also left his mark.

We direct that a copy of this expression be spread of record in the Order Book of the Wabash Circuit Court, that a copy be forwarded to the family and to the Supreme Court of Indiana, and a copy retained in the files of the Wabash County Bar Association.

Sarah Kelton Browne
Lynn A. Ford
John W. Beauchamp
Charles R. Tiede
William H. Tallman
Donald R. Metz
Robert E. Bostwick
J. W. Daggett
Robert R. McCadlen
A. H. Plummer III
Robert E. Magley
Robert F. Gonderman
J. Ward Vandegrift
        Members, Wabash County
        Bar Association

Photo courtesy of Manuscript Section, Indiana State Library.

Charles W. Cook, Jr.

1906-1968

- Born January 26, 1906, in Indianapolis, Marion County, Indiana.
- Served as a law clerk to Willis C. McMahan and Charles F. Remy, both judges of the Indiana Appellate Court, while in law school.
- Began a lengthy career as a civil trial lawyer in 1929.
- Served as general counsel for the Indiana Toll Road Commission from 1952 to 1959.
- Served as a delegate to the Republican National Convention in 1960.
- Elected to the Indiana Court of Appeals in 1966, serving until his death.
- Died November 21, 1968, in Indianapolis, Marion County, Indiana.

IN THE SUPREME COURT OF INDIANA
1968 TERM
ORDER OF ADJOURNMENT IN MEMORIAM OF
OUR JUDICIAL COLLEAGUE AND ASSOCIATE JUDGE
OF THE APPELLATE COURT OF INDIANA

WHEREAS, This Court is extremely distressed at the announcement of the untimely passing of our Judicial Colleague, Charles W. Cook, Jr., Associate Justice of the Appellate Court of Indiana, a distinguished member of said Court, and an outstanding public servant; and

WHEREAS, his outstanding career as a lawyer in Marion County, Indiana and as a Judge of the Appellate Court are exemplified in his unique and penetrating grasp of legal principles as recorded in his written opinions of said Court;

WHEREAS, his colleagues on the Appellate Court and his Judicial Colleagues on the Supreme Court have lost an outstanding jurist, and the Bench and Bar of this State have lost an outstanding lawyer and jurist; and,

WHEREAS, his untimely death will be felt by the Bench and Bar of this State for many years to come;

NOW THEREFORE BE IT RESOLVED AND ORDERED that the Supreme Court of Indiana stand adjourned in memoriam of the Honorable Charles W. Cook, Jr., a brother Judge, from 12:00 Noon, Friday November 22, 1968 until 1:00 P.M., Monday, November 24, 1968 and the Clerk of this Court is directed to spread this order IN MEMORIAM on the records of this Court and transmit a copy hereof to his bereaved widow, Gene, sons, James M. and G. Michael, and grandchildren, all of which is done this 21st day of November, 1968, at 4:00 P.M.

Donald H. Hunter
Acting Chief Justice

Witness the seal of this Court,
this 21st day of November, 1968.

xliv

Amos Wade Jackson
1904-1972

- Born June 25, 1904, in Versailles, Ripley County, Indiana.

- Received a bachelor's degree from Hanover College (Hanover, Indiana) in 1926.

- Admitted to the Indiana bar in 1925, while a senior in college.

- Served as Ripley County Prosecuting Attorney from 1937 to 1940.

- Served as an associate attorney for the United States Army Corps of Engineers during World War II.

- Appointed to the Indiana Supreme Court in 1959, serving from January 5, 1959, until January 4, 1971, when he retired for health reasons.

- Died September 30, 1972, in Madison, Jefferson County, Indiana.

In Memoriam

MEMORIAL RESOLUTION
OF THE
RIPLEY COUNTY BAR ASSOCIATION
ON THE DEATH OF
AMOS W. JACKSON

WHEREAS, the Honorable Amos W. Jackson passed away at the King's Daughters' Hospital at Madison, Indiana, on September 30, 1972, and,

THEREFORE, these resolutions of respect are prepared for adoption by the Ripley County Bar Association.

Amos W. Jackson was a lifelong resident of Ripley County, he was born on June 25, 1904, the son of Rowland H. Jackson, a lawyer and member of the Ripley County Bar, and Georgia Frohliger. He attended the Versailles Schools, graduated from the Versailles High School, and from Hanover College in 1926. He was admitted to the Ripley County Bar in September, 1925. He served as Prosecuting Attorney of Ripley County for two terms from 1937 to 1940 and also served as Ripley County Probation Officer. He served as an assistant attorney to the United States Attorney General in 1942 and 1943. In 1930 he formed a partnership with his father in the general practice of law at Versailles under the firm name of Jackson and Jackson, which continued until his father's death.

In 1958 he was elected a member of the Indiana Supreme Court and served in that capacity for two six-year terms from 1959 to 1970. In 1964 he was honored by Hanover College with a Distinguished Alumni Award. He suffered ill health for the last two or three years of his life and was unable to re-establish his law practice in Versailles after leaving the Supreme Court Bench.

xxxii

RULES OF SUPREME COURT. xxxiii

On August 20, 1927, he was married to Lola Raper and is survived by his widow and one daughter, Mrs. Ann Louise Stanley of Indianapolis.

Judge Jackson was a member of the Indiana Judges Association, the American, Indiana, Ripley County and Indianapolis Bar Associations and Masonic Lodge No. 7 and Chapter 333 of the Order of Eastern Star, both of Versailles.

THEREFORE, BE IT RESOLVED by the Ripley County Bar Association in special memorial session, that in the passing of Amos W. Jackson the legal profession in Indiana has lost a distinguished jurist, the Ripley County Bar Association has lost a distinguished member and the citizens of Versailles and Ripley County have lost a valued and distinguished citizen.

BE IT FURTHER RESOLVED that a copy of these resolutions be spread of record on the Civil Order Book of the Ripley Circuit Court, and that copies be furnished to Mrs. Lola Jackson and Mrs. Ann Louise Stanley.

Adopted this 4th day of October, 1972.

> Ripley County Bar Association
> By its Memorial Committee
> WILLIAM J. SCHRODER, Judge
> PHILLIPS B. JOHNSON
> PAUL V. WYCOFF

STATE OF INDIANA ⎫
RIPLEY COUNTY ⎬ ss:

I, Beverly J. Speer, Clerk of the Ripley Circuit Court, in and for said County and State aforesaid, do hereby certify that the above and foregoing is a true and correct copy of MEMORIAL RESOLUTION OF THE RIPLEY COUNTY BAR ASSOCIATION ON THE DEATH OF AMOS W. JACKSON in Cause No. ———, In the Matter of ——————————— as the same appears of record in Civil Order Book No. 0000 at page 341, in this office, and of which I am legal custodian.

xxxiv   RULES OF SUPREME COURT.

IN WITNESS WHEREOF, I have hereunto subscribed my name and affixed the official seal of said Court at Versailles, Indiana, this 20th day of December, 1972.

BEVERLY J. SPEER,
Clerk Ripley Circuit Court

Portrait courtesy of Walter H. Palmer, Judge, Gibson Circuit Court, Princeton, Indiana.

Harvey W. Garrett

1901-1976

- Born November 9, 1901, in Patoka, Gibson County, Indiana.

- Received a bachelor's degree from Indiana University in 1928.

- Admitted to the bar in 1931, practicing law in Owensville, Gibson County, Indiana.

- Practiced law in Princeton, Gibson County, Indiana, from 1936 until 1965.

- Appointed Gibson Circuit Court judge in 1965 after the death of Judge Dale Eby.

- Elected to six-year terms as circuit court judge in both 1966 and 1972.

- Died April 14, 1976, in Evansville, Vanderburgh County, Indiana.

In Memoriam

HARVEY M. GARRETT
1901 - 1976

On April 14, 1976, at 9:35 P.M. the Creator saw fit to take from our midst a beloved and respected citizen of this community and a member of the Gibson County Bar, Judge Harvey W. Garrett.

Harvey W. Garrett was born on November 9, 1901, in Patoka, Indiana, the son of Henry Garrett and Louise Wilson Garrett.

He attended the public schools of Gibson County and was graduated from Indiana University. In 1931 he began the practice of law at Owensville, Indiana, served two terms as Prosecuting Attorney of the 66th Judicial Circuit and continued the active practice of law until his appointment to the Circuit Judgeship of the Gibson Circuit Court in September, 1965.

Judge Garrett married Virginia Welburn and to this union were born three children: Richard W. Garrett, Joseph Garrett and Rebecca Garrett.

Judge Garrett was an extremely considerate husband and devoted father and above all else his family was his pride and joy.

Judge Garrett was a member of the National College of Probate Judges, The American Judicature Society, The Indiana Judges Association, The Gibson County Bar Association, The Indiana State Bar Association, The Princeton Kiwanis Club, Masonic Lodge, The Princeton Country Club, Advisory Board of the Salvation Army and an Elder in the Broadway Christian Church.

In his capacity as Judge, Harvey was honest, fair, patient, stern but compassionate.

He expected and maintained absolute dignity and decorum in his Courtroom.

It is by no means intended that these few brief remarks should be a complete summation of Judge Garrett's career and life.

If there ever existed a person who understood the value, purpose and meaning of life it was Harvey W. Garrett.

He loved his Country, his flag, and his Bible with a fervent passion.

Posted conspicuously in his chambers were the Ten Commandments and a Poem "What Our Flag Means To Me".

We all feel a great sense of personal loss at Judge Garrett's passing. We shall miss him, and appreciate that this world is a better place because Judge Harvey W. Garrett has lived among us.

THEREFORE, BE IT RESOLVED that the Gibson County, Indiana Bar Association give a public expression of the sorrow of its members on the death of Judge Harvey W. Garrett.

BE IT FURTHER RESOLVED that a copy of this Resolution be transmitted to the widow and children of Judge Garrett.

BE IT FURTHER RESOLVED that this Resolution be placed of record in the permanent records of the Gibson Circuit Court and that a copy thereof be certified to the Indiana Supreme Court with a request that the same be spread of record and ordered published in the Indiana Reports.

Respectfully submitted,

Signed: GIBSON COUNTY BAR ASSOCIATION

George J. Ankenbrand	Dan L. Reeves	Bruce D. McDonald
Robert J. Fair	Jerry D. Stilwell	Loren G. McGregor
Mark P. Lockwood	Arthur S. Wilson	Charles R. Nixon
William J. Marshall	Tom Dike	Verner P. Partenheimer, Jr.
James G. McDonald, Jr.	John W. Ballard	George R. Rehnquist
Maurice B. Miller	Gerald E. Hall	Leon C. Stone
Walter H. Palmer	David C. Luecking	Virginia O'Leary

lxxii   IN MEMORIAM.

STATE OF INDIANA ⎫
                      ⎬ SS:
COUNTY OF GIBSON ⎭

I, the undersigned Clerk of the Gibson Circuit Court of said County, hereby certify that the above and foregoing instrument consisting of one page is a copy of the In Memoriam made and entered in Gibson Circuit Court on the 19th day of April 1976.

Witness My Hand and Official Seal this the 18th day of May, 1976.

(SEAL)   RUSSELL KERN, *Clerk*
                              NANCY J. THOMAS, *Deputy*

Archie "Arch" Newton Bobbitt

〜 1895-1978 〜

- Born September 3, 1895, in Eckerty, Crawford County, Indiana.

- Attended Central Normal College (Danville, Indiana).

- Began his professional career as a school teacher and principal.

- Elected Crawford County Clerk in 1918, but resigned in order to join the Navy during World War I.

- Served as the Crawford County Auditor from 1921 to 1925, and as a gasoline tax collector from 1925 to 1929.

- Received a law degree from Benjamin Harrison Law School (now Indiana School of Law—Indianapolis) in 1927.

- Elected to the post of State Auditor where he uncovered a gasoline bootlegging scheme and recovered evaded taxes.

- Returned to private law practice in 1930.

Continued 〜

Archie "Arch" Newton Bobbitt

 continued

- Returned to public office as an Indianapolis city attorney from 1943 to 1948, serving as the chief city attorney from 1945 to 1948.

- Elected to the Indiana Supreme Court in 1950.

- Became chief justice the day he took his seat on the court (January 1, 1951) due to court rules concerning the rotation of the chief justice position.

- Served on the Indiana Supreme Court until January 7, 1963, when defeated in re-election by Walter Myers, Jr.

- Returned to private law practice in his former firm, Ruckelhaus, Bobbitt & O'Connor.

- Died January 24, 1978, in Indianapolis, Marion County, Indiana.

In Memoriam

1895 — 1978

Judge Arch N. Bobbitt died January 24, 1978 in Indianapolis, Indiana. He was born at Eckerty, Indiana, September 3, 1895, to Ida Newton Bobbitt and Irvin Bobbitt.

A native of Eckerty in Crawford County, Judge Bobbitt was a graduate of the nearby Birdseye High School. He attended the former Central Normal College, Danville, Indiana, and received his law degree from Indiana University Law School.

Judge Bobbitt taught school in Crawford County one year and then was principal of Alton High School one year and Marengo High School two years. He was elected clerk of Crawford County in 1918, but resigned to enter the Navy and served in World War I. After the war, he taught in Crawford County and in 1920 was elected to a four-year term as Crawford County auditor. At the same time, he served as Republican County Chairman and later was elected as Third District Chairman.

As district chairman, he soon became active in State politics and in 1925 was appointed director of the State gasoline tax department, a position he held until 1928 when he was elected to a two-year term as State auditor. He entered law practice in Indianapolis in 1930.

Judge Bobbitt became State GOP chairman in 1937 and was re-elected to two two-year terms in 1938 and 1940. He was attorney for the City of Indianapolis from 1943 to 1944, and was chief city attorney from 1945 to 1948.

In November, 1950, Judge Bobbitt was elected to the Supreme Court of Indiana and took office January 1, 1951, and served until January, 1963. He became Chief Justice the day he took his oath of office due to the then prevailing standing

xxxvii

xxxviii   IN MEMORIAM.

rule of the court which rotated the court's top position automatically by districts.

From 1963 until his death, he was the senior partner with the firm of Ruckelshaus, Bobbitt & O'Connor. Judge Bobbitt, meanwhile, had become a senior adviser to Republican politicians.

In 1972 The Bobbs-Merrill Company, Inc. published Judge Bobbitt's two-volume treatise on Indiana Appellate Practice and Procedure. He also authored Bobbitt's Revision of Work's Indiana Practice.

He was a member of the American Legion, the 40 & 8, Meridian Street United Methodist Church; and a fifty-year member of the Masonic Lodge at Eckerty, Indiana, the Scottish Rite, and the Hadi Temple at Evansville.

He also was a member of the Indianapolis, Indiana, and American Bar Associations, Sigma Delta Kappa Legal Fraternity, Service Club of Indianapolis and the Indiana Society of Chicago.

In 1975 he was honored as a fifty-year member of the Columbia Club; and as a fifty-year member of The Indianapolis Bar Association. A group of lawyers belonging to the Indianapolis Law School Alumni Association purchased a portrait of Judge Bobbitt painted by a prominent artist, Edmund Brucker, and presented it to Indiana University where it now hangs. Judge Bobbitt was also a life member of the House of Delegates of the Indiana State Bar Association.

Judge Bobbitt was listed in Who's Who in America; Who's Who Among Authors and Journalists; Who's Who in Law; and Who's Who in the World.

Upon his death Governor Otis R. Bowen said,

> "Mr. Bobbitt was an outstanding gentleman who compiled a lengthy and distinguished record of public service to both Government and the Republican Party. He will be missed by all who knew him."

Attorney General Theodore L. Sendak said of Judge Bobbitt,

IN MEMORIAM. xxxix

"He had an understanding of human nature I haven't found in many people, bridging the gap between several generations. He had a kind of sparkle—he was a great man."

Judge Allen Sharp of the United States District Court for the Northern District of Indiana said of Judge Bobbitt,

"There was a personal characteristic that I admired so greatly. He had been deeply involved in politics since 1920. He had achieved much and had sustained some major disappointments. In it all he had never become bitter and cynical. He prided himself in helping those of us who were younger. Arch Bobbitt led a long and useful life that was a benefit to his profession, State and Country."

Many men are born imbued with a deep love of liberty. More rarely, but still frequently, they come into this world possessed of an instinctive intense dislike of injustice. Much more rarely, they have that fine sense of perception and logical analysis which is referred to as the "legal mind" and which invariably marks the great lawyer. When all of these qualities happen to be combined in one man, we have a great Judge. Judge Bobbitt possessed these qualities; they made him a great Judge. Though partisan, he knew no prejudices. He believed in the American way of life and the Bill of Rights. His monument, more enduring than bronze or stone, is built of his well-reasoned opinions which appear in the Reports of the Supreme Court of Indiana and that monument will stand to attest his greatness and point the way of oncoming generations of lawyers and Judges to the just application of the rules and principles of the law.

Judge Bobbitt was a successful lawyer, an able Judge, a fair and kind man and a good American.

We extend our sympathy to his widow Frances A. Bobbitt; his sister Mae (Mrs. Paul B.) Ringham; his nieces, Jean (Mrs. Ronald) Alley, and Barbara (Mrs. Frank) Miller; and his nephews Thomas Bobbitt, Reverend Lester Ringham and William Ringham.

ADOPTION OF MEMORIAL RESOLUTION
OF THE
SUPREME COURT OF INDIANA
IN MEMORY OF THE LATE
HONORABLE ARCH N. BOBBITT

ORDER

The Court orders the foregoing Memorial Resolution spread of record upon the permanent records of this Court, and the Clerk of this Court is ordered to deliver a copy of said Memorial Resolution to the Reporter of this Court who is ordered to print and publish the same in the official Reports of the Supreme Court of Indiana.

The Court acknowledges with appreciation the assistance of Wideha (Mrs. Russell P.) Stott, who was Judge Bobbitt's secretary during his tenure as Judge of the Supreme Court of Indiana, in the preparation of said Memorial Resolution.

IT IS FURTHER ORDERED that the Clerk of this Court transmit a copy of said Memorial Resolution, under the Seal of this Court, to the widow of the late Honorable Arch N. Bobbitt, Mrs. Frances A. Bobbitt, and to his sister, Mrs. Paul B. Ringham.

IT IS FURTHER ORDERED that the Clerk of this Court transmit a copy of said Memorial Resolution to the Clerk of the Crawford County Circuit Court, English, Indiana, who is instructed to spread said Memorial Resolution of record.

DONE at Indianapolis, Indiana, this 29th day of March, 1978.

Richard M. Givan, Chief Justice
Supreme Court of Indiana

xl

Norman Frank Arterburn

⁓ 1902-1979 ⁓

- Born May 13, 1902, in Bicknell, Knox County, Indiana.

- Received a bachelor's degree from Indiana University in 1923.

- Admitted to practice law the same year he graduated from college.

- Received a law degree from the University of Chicago in 1926.

- Taught at Washburn College (Topeka, Kansas) in 1926 and 1927.

- Practiced law in Vincennes, Knox County, Indiana, from 1927 to 1955.

- Was a member of the Indiana Board of Law Examiners from 1938 to 1944.

- Taught at Indiana University in 1949, 1953, and 1954.

- Appointed to the Indiana Supreme Court in 1955, serving from May 23, 1955, to May 13, 1977.

Continued ⁓

Norman Frank Arterburn

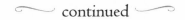 continued

- Selected as the court's first permanent chief justice, a process changed by the 1970 amending of the Indiana Constitution, and remained in that position until 1974.
- Died February 10, 1979, in Florida.

IN MEMORIAM

1902-1979

JUSTICE NORMAN F. ARTERBURN was Born May 13, 1902. He died February 10, 1979, in Fort Myers, Florida. He left surviving him his widow, Loretta Vieck Arterburn, three daughters, Joan Arterburn of Vincennes, Faith Nicholson of Route 3, Vincennes and Linda Ridgley of Pueblo, Colorado. He is also survived by seven grandchildren and two sisters, Thelma Arterburn and Constance Smith, both of Athens, Tennessee. He was preceded in death by his first wife, Lois Richards Arterburn, and a daughter, Joyce. His parents, the late Clay H. and Anna Hoover Arterburn, and his brother, Lowell Arterburn, also preceded him in death.

JUSTICE ARTERBURN was the first Chief Justice of Indiana under the 1971 judicial amendment. He served as Chief Justice until November 1974, when he retired from that position. He remained on the Court until his retirement from the bench on May 13, 1977, after 22 years of service on the Indiana Supreme Court. His experience in the fields of jurisprudence encompassed the general practice in semi-rural county seat communities, the teaching of law and service upon the highest court of Indiana.

He was a native Hoosier, the son of a Hoosier schoolteacher. He and his brother, Lowell, alternately taught school to help each other through college. In 1923, JUSTICE ARTERBURN graduated with honors from Indiana University, then studied one year on the Bloomington campus before enrolling in the University of Chicago Law School, where he received his law degree. From law school in Chicago he moved to Topeka, Kansas and taught law at Washburn University Law School. Returning to Vincennes, he entered into the private practice with the late C. B. Kessinger and W. H. Hill, and finally with Arthur L. Hart. He served for a time as a visiting professor of law at Indiana University Law School while practicing in Indiana. He served one term

xxix

xxx   IN MEMORIAM.

as Prosecuting Attorney of Knox County, Indiana. In 1955 he was appointed to the Indiana Supreme Court by Governor George N. Craig. In 1956 he was elected to a full term and was re-elected continually thereafter until his retirement at the age of 75 years.

When JUSTICE ARTERBURN joined the Court in 1955 each Judge had a backlog of one hundred or more cases. Under his inspiring leadership the Court became current in its work, aggressively moving forward in many areas to improve the administration of justice. He firmly believed in the courts expediting the disposition of litigation and promptly hearing all matters before them. He was impatient with delay and took every opportunity to eliminate the causes therefor.

JUSTICE ARTERBURN was a participant in the development of jurisdictional authority of the Supreme Court over local trial courts, expansion of the Court of Appeals and its jurisdiction and improvement of standards for the education and examination of candidates for admission to the law profession. He was the catalyst which precipiated the adoption of new procedural rules expediting the work of all the courts. He was in the forefront of the successful struggle leading to the adoption of effective procedures for the discipline of lawyers who did not measure up to the high standards of the legal profession.

He was particularly proud of the Supreme Court and its members for their continual effort to improve the judicial system. JUSTICE ARTERBURN recognized that the law was a jealous mistress. He believed in the legal profession. In spite of the everyday pressing demands experienced by the legal profession in the performance of its duties, he still felt a deep and abiding regard for the law. He once said: "I love the law. If it were not for the law, we would not have society. A lawyer settles the conflicts, the differences among people. The judiciary does it and does it in a peaceable manner . . . and I say lawyers are the great social workers. They may not realize this, but they are the great social workers that cement society and keep it operating peaceably."

IN MEMORIAM. xxxi

He was a great believer in law and order. He contended that the members of society should restrain themselves in such a manner that individuals might live side by side in an orderly society. Accordingly, he insisted upon appropriate restraints upon the individual to the end that society would progress. In a court opinion written by him, he stated: "Absolute and unlimited freedom in a society is only the reverse side of the coin of anarchy. No government of law and order would be possible under the doctrine of unlimited freedoms."

JUSTICE ARTERBURN was an avid golfer. He worked at such game with the same dedication and intensity as he did the practice of law and his work on the Indiana Supreme Court. He was a perfectionist in everything that he did, insisting that an individual should continually improve himself in order that whatever he might be doing he would be doing it to the best of his ability. Accordingly, he was stern with himself with the result that hours upon hours were spent in his work on the Court which he might otherwise have spent in enjoying the golf game that he so much loved.

He was a family man and was deeply concerned about the welfare of his children. This concern evidenced itself in his daily living as he always found time to interest himself in their affairs, but solely and only for the purpose of advantaging them in their daily activities and in their lives.

JUSTICE ARTERBURN was a man of intense loyalty. He recognized that true friendships were few and far between and, accordingly, when he extended his friendship to another it was a friendship that was rarely, if ever, broken or splintered. He had very little time for fair-weather friends or those who would use others and discard them after they had served their purpose.

He always had concern for the disadvantaged. He gave of his substance to help others and did it unstintingly and without outside pressures.

As an educator he was proud of the growth of Vincennes University. Quietly and often unnoticed he lent his influence

xxxii   IN MEMORIAM.

to the advantage of the University, recognizing that for many years last past it had not been accorded the position in the State that rightfully belonged to it. In at least one legal opinion written by him he recognized that it was a public institution and a part of the State educational system. He was particularly pleased as the years went by that Vincennes University was recognized as one of the great junior colleges of America and often said that such proved his early and abiding faith in it. He was glad that the people of Indiana had recognized, by their support of the University, the great heritage that they had retained by so doing and the opportunities that they were giving students to learn and become good citizens when otherwise such probably, in many instances, would not have been their lot.

JUSTICE ARTERBURN was a member of the First United Methodist Church, Vincennes. He was past president of Vincennes Kiwanis Club, Chamber of Commerce, Board of Governors of Good Samaritan Hospital and Vincennes Country Club. He was a member of the Knox County Bar Association, Indiana State Bar Association and the American Bar Association.

ADOPTION OF MEMORIAL RESOLUTION
OF THE
SUPREME COURT OF INDIANA
IN MEMORY OF THE LATE
HONORABLE NORMAN F. ARTERBURN

ORDER

The Court orders the foregoing Memorial Resolution spread of record upon the permanent records of this Court. The Clerk of this Court is ordered to deliver a copy of said Memorial Resolution to the Reporter of this Court, who is ordered to print and publish the same in the official Reports of the Supreme Court of Indiana.

The Court acknowledges with appreciation the assistance in the preparation of said Memorial Resolution of Arthur L.

IN MEMORIAM. xxxiii

Hart of Vincennes, Indiana, who was Justice Arterburn's law partner and close friend.

IT IS FURTHER ORDERED that the Clerk of this Court transmit a copy of said Memorial Resolution, under the Seal of this Court, to the widow of the late Honorable Norman F. Arterburn, Mrs. Loretta V. Arterburn; to his three daughters, Joan Arterburn, Faith Nicholson and Linda Ridgley; to his two sisters, Thelma Arterburn and Constance Smith; and to Arthur L. Hart.

IT IS FURTHER ORDERED that the Clerk of this Court transmit a copy of said Memorial Resolution to the Clerk of the Knox Circuit Court, Vincennes, Indiana, who is instructed to spread said Memorial Resolution of record.

DONE at Indianapolis, Indiana, this 19th day of June, 1979.

Richard M. Givan
Chief Justice of Indiana

Floyd S. Draper

1893-1980

- Born October 17, 1893, in Fulton, New York.

- Received his legal education at Valparaiso (Valparaiso, Indiana) University Law School, graduating with honors in 1915.

- Began public service when he became chief deputy prosecutor for Lake County, Indiana, in 1923.

- Served as city attorney for Gary, Lake County, Indiana, in 1939.

- Elected to the Indiana Court of Appeals in 1942.

- Re-elected to the Court of Appeals in 1946.

- Served in the Indiana Supreme Court from January 2, 1951, to January 10, 1955, resigning a year before the expiration of his term because of his brother's poor health.

- Retired from legal practice in 1958, but accepted an appointment to the Lake County Criminal Court from Governor Hadley in 1960.

- Died March 20, 1980, in Bradenton, Florida.

IN MEMORIAM
1893-1980

Judge Floyd S. Draper died March 20, 1980, in Bradenton, Florida, where he and Mrs. Draper retired in the 1960s.

Judge Draper was born in Fulton, New York. He was a longtime resident of Gary, Indiana, and was elected as a Republican to the Court of Appeals of Indiana in 1942 and reelected in 1946. In 1950 he was elected to the Supreme Court of Indiana, where he served with distinction until 1955 when he resigned a year before his term expired because of the health of his brother, the late Alfred P. Draper. Upon his resignation he returned to Gary and practiced law with his brother and son, the late John M. Draper.

At the time of his death the Gary Post Tribune published the following editorial:

"Any attorney who devoted as much time to public service as did Floyd S. Draper would deserve the attention of his fellow citizens at the time of his passing.

"But with Draper, who died at 86 in Florida last week, there was an added reason for remembering a particular chapter of his government service.

"In 1958, Draper retired, having already served as a deputy prosecutor, a city attorney, in judgeships on both the Supreme and Appellate Courts of Indiana, and then three years in private practice.

"Two years later, however, when Judge William J. Murray died in office, Draper heeded the call of Gov. Harold Handley and returned to active service on the Lake Criminal Court.

"Whether he did it out of Republican loyalty, he and Handley being GOP activists, or out of a desire to restore more faith to the Lake County judicial system (and we prefer the latter version) it was the action of a man possessed of a keen sense of duty.

"In general, judicial offices pay less than capable attorneys can make in private practice—certainly than Draper had made in his post-judicial practice here. Many attorneys now take such posts to further their own careers and then open private offices to profit

xxxi

on their reputations. In a sense, Draper had done that — and then happily retired.

"Yet, when another call came he answered it. We need citizens with that sort of sense of duty."

Judge Draper was a 1915 graduate of Valparaiso University Law School, where he graduated with honors. He entered public service in 1923 when he became chief deputy prosecutor for Lake County. In 1939 he served as city attorney for Gary.

He was a member of Sigma Delta Kappa Legal Fraternity; First Presbyterian Church of Merrillville, Indiana; Gary Masonic Lodge; Indiana State and American Bar Associations; and a life member of the Gary Bar Association, now Lake County Bar Association. Judge Draper is listed in Who's Who in America; and is mentioned at some length by historian Richard S. Kaplan in his book, "History of the Gary Bar Association 1921 to 1949."

Judge Draper was beloved by all who knew him. He had a capacity for many friendships. The members of the Bench and Bar will remember him for his keen and brilliant mind which is reflected in his many well-reasoned and scholarly opinions in the Indiana Reports of our two highest State Courts. He possessed a great humility, a keen sense of humor, and an intense desire for fairness to all mankind, regardless of race, creed or color. He felt a deep and abiding love for his country and was, in the finest sense, a great American and an outstanding credit to the legal profession as a capable lawyer and a very able jurist.

We extend our sympathy to his daughter-in-law Janet Draper (Mrs. Robert) Nutt, and his grandsons Jeffrey A. Draper, John M. Draper, Jr. and Joel K. Draper.

ADOPTION OF MEMORIAL RESOLUTION
OF THE
SUPREME COURT OF INDIANA
IN MEMORY OF THE LATE HONORABLE FLOYD S. DRAPER

ORDER

The Court orders the foregoing Memorial Resolution spread of record

IN MEMORIAM   xxxiii

upon the permanent records of this Court, and the Clerk of this Court is ordered to deliver a copy of said Memorial Resolution to the Reporter of this Court who is ordered to print and publish the same in the official Reports of the Supreme Court of Indiana.

IT IS FURTHER ORDERED that the Clerk of this Court transmit a copy of said Memorial Resolution, under the seal of this Court, to JUDGE DRAPER'S daughter-in-law Janet Draper (Mrs. Robert) Nutt of Merrillville, Indiana; and his grandsons Jeffrey A. Draper of Merrillville, Indiana; John M. Draper, Jr., of Vacaville, California; and Joel K. Draper of Greensburg, Indiana.

IT IS FURTHER ORDERED that the Clerk of this Court transmit a copy of said Memorial Resolution to the Clerk of the Lake Circuit Court, Crown Point, Indiana, who is instructed to spread said Memorial Resolution of record.

DONE at Indianapolis, Indiana, this 12th day of March, 1981.

> Richard M. Givan, Chief Justice
> Supreme Court of Indiana

MEMORIAL RESOLUTION
OF THE
LAKE COUNTY BAR ASSOCIATION

IN MEMORIAM
HONORABLE FLOYD S. DRAPER

1893-1980

Judge Floyd S. Draper died March 20, 1980, in Bradenton, Florida where he and Mrs. Draper retired in the 1960s.

Judge Draper was born in Fulton, New York. He was a longtime resident of Gary, Indiana, and was elected as a Republican to the Court of Appeal of Indiana in 1942 and reelected in 1946. In 1950 he was elected to the Supreme Court of Indiana, where he served with distinction until 1955, when he resigned a year before his term expired because of the health of his brother, the late Alfred P. Draper. Upon his resignation he returned to Gary and practiced law with his brother and son, the late John M. Draper.

At the time of his death the Gary Post Tribune published the following editorial:

HE CAME BACK WHEN NEEDED

Any attorney who devoted as much time to public service as did Floyd S. Draper would deserve the attention of his fellow citizens at the time of his passing.

But with Draper, who died at 86 in Florida last week, there was an added reason for remembering a particular chapter of his government service.

In 1958, Draper retired, having already served as a deputy prosecutor, a city attorney, in judgeships on both the Supreme and Appellate Courts of Indiana, and then three years in private practice.

Two years later, however, when Judge William J. Murray died in office, Draper heeded the call of Gov. Harold Handley and returned to active service on the Lake Criminal Court.

Whether he did it out of Republican loyalty, he and Handley being GOP activists, or out of a desire to restore more faith to the Lake County judicial system (and we prefer the latter version) it was the action of a man possessed of a keen sense of duty.

In general, judicial offices pay less than capable attorneys can make in private practice — certainly than Draper had made in his postjudicial practice here. Many attorneys now take such posts to further their own careers and then open private offices to profit on their reputations. In a sense, Draper had done that — and then happily retired.

Yet, when another call came he answered it. We need citizens with that sort of sense of duty.

Judge Draper was a 1915 graduate of Valparaiso University of Law School, where he graduated with honors. He entered public service in 1923 when he became chief deputy prosecutor for Lake County. In 1939 he served as city attorney for Gary.

He was a member of Sigma Delta Kappa Legal Fraternity; First Presbyterian Church of Merrillville, Indiana; Gary Masonic Lodge; In-

IN MEMORIAM   xxxv

diana State and American Bar Associations; and a life member of the
Gary Bar Association, now Lake County Bar Association. Judge Draper
is listed in Who's Who in America; and is mentioned at some length
by historian Richard S. Kaplan in his book, "History of the Gary Bar
Association 1921 to 1949."

Judge Draper was beloved by all who knew him. He had a capacity
for many friendships. The members of the Bench and Bar will remember
him for his keen and brilliant mind which is reflected in his many well-
reasoned and scholarly opinions in the Indiana Reports of our two highest
State courts. He possessed great humility, and keen sense of humor,
and an intense desire for fairness to all mankind, regardless of race,
creed or color. He felt a deep and abiding love for his country and was,
in the finest sense, a great American and an outstanding credit to the
legal profession as a capable lawyer and a very able jurist.

We extend our sympathy to his daughter-in-law Janet Draper (Mrs.
Robert) Nutt, and his grandsons Jeffrey A. Draper, John M. Draper,
Jr. and Joel K. Draper.

Be it resolved that a copy of this Resolution be transmitted to the
daughter-in-law and grandsons of Judge Floyd S. Draper.

Be it further resolved that this Resolution be placed of record in the
permanent records of the Court of Lake County, Indiana.

> Respectfully submitted,
> Lake County Bar Association
> Harry A. Psimos
> President, Lake County Bar Association

IN THE
SUPREME COURT OF INDIANA

ORDER

The Lake County Bar Association, having adopted a MEMORIAL
RESOLUTION in memory of The Honorable Floyd S. Draper, former
Judge of the Supreme Court and Court of Appeals, and having filed the

xxxvi **IN MEMORIAM**

same in open court in the Lake Circuit Court, now tenders same for filing with the Supreme Court of Indiana.

IT IS, THEREFORE, ORDERED that said Memorial Resolution be spread of record in the Supreme Court of the State of Indiana.

DATED: May 11, 1981.

Richard M. Givan
Chief Justice of Indiana

Portrait courtesy of the Indiana Court of Appeals.

John W. Pfaff

∽ 1901-1977 ∽

- Born February 26, 1901, in Marietta, Ohio.

- Graduated from Hanover (Hanover, Indiana) College in 1926.

- Graduated from the Indianapolis Law School and admitted to the Indiana bar in 1929.

- Practiced law in South Bend, St. Joesph County, Indiana, from 1929 until 1954.

- Served as an assistant to the Indiana Superior Court and on the staff of the United States District Attorney.

- Elected to the Indiana Court of Appeals in 1954, serving for twelve years.

- Died February 27, 1977, in Edwardsburg, Michigan.

𝕸𝖊𝖒𝖔𝖗𝖎𝖆𝖑 𝕽𝖊𝖘𝖔𝖑𝖚𝖙𝖎𝖔𝖓

for

THE HONORABLE JOHN W. PFAFF

Chief Justice, Appellate Court of Indiana

*

XLIII

357–360 N.E. 2d xliii (Ind. Ct. App. 1977)

In Memoriam

The following Resolution was adopted as a Memorial to the late John W. Pfaff.

WHEREAS, the Honorable John W. Pfaff of Eagle Lake, Edwardsburg, Michigan, a previous resident of South Bend, Indiana, was a former Chief Justice of the Appellate Court of Indiana; and

WHEREAS, it is with deep regret that we note the passing of Judge Pfaff on February 27, 1977, whose active and useful life spanned 76 years; and

WHEREAS, Judge Pfaff was elected to the Appellate Court of Indiana in 1954 for a four-year term, and elected in 1960 to a second four-year term, and again elected in 1966 to a third four-year term; and

WHEREAS, he served as Chief Justice of the Appellate Court of Indiana in 1967 and 1969; and

WHEREAS, Judge Pfaff was a native of Marietta, Ohio, and he came to Indiana at an early age, and graduated from Hanover College in 1926, and graduated from the former Indianapolis Law School, and was admitted to practice in 1929; and

WHEREAS, he began the general practice of law in South Bend following graduation from law school, and served on the staff of the U. S. District Attorney, and took leave from his law firm upon being elected Judge of the Appellate Court in 1954; and

XLV

IN MEMORIAM

WHEREAS, Judge Pfaff was past master of Portage Lodge 675, Free and Accepted Masons, and a 32nd Degree Mason, and a member of the Saint Joseph County Bar Association, and a member of the Indiana State Bar Association, and a member of Beta Theta Pi Law fraternity; and

WHEREAS, he had been a member of the Scottish Rite, Murat Temple Shrine, the Kiwanis Club, Ridgedale Presbyterian Church, and was active in the Community Chest, Red Cross and Boy Scout Organizations; and

WHEREAS, he served the State of Indiana with distinction during his twelve years as Judge of the Appellate Court of Indiana. He was energetic in the discharge of his duties; and had an intense interest in matters pertaining to the conduct of the court; and was always courteous and considerate to the lawyers appearing before him; and his warm and friendly personality will live on for many years in the memories of his friends; and

WHEREAS, he leaves surviving: his widow, Odessa W.; two sons, John W. Pfaff of Fairfax, Virginia and Robert A. Pfaff of Elkhart, Indiana, and eight grandchildren; and

WHEREAS, his passing is a great loss to his community, our State, his family and friends.

BE IT RESOLVED, that this Memorial Resolution be adopted by the Court of Appeals of Indiana and spread of record on the Order Books of this Court, and that the Clerk of this Court is ordered to deliver a copy of this Memorial Resolution to the Reporter of this Court, who is ordered to print and publish the same in the Indiana Court of Appeals Reports.

BE IT FURTHER RESOLVED, that the members of this Court extend their sympathy to the widow, sons and family, and friends of this able lawyer and Jurist; and that a copy of this Memorial Resolution be spread upon the records of the Saint Joseph Circuit Court, at South Bend, Indiana; and that a copy of this Memorial Resolution, under the seal of this Court, be sent

HONORABLE JOHN W. PFAFF

to his widow, Mrs. Odessa W. Pfaff, at Rural Route 3, Box 209–480, Lakeview Drive, Eagle Lake, Edwardsburg, Michigan, 49112.

DONE at Indianapolis, Indiana, this fourteenth day of March, 1977.

/s/ Jonathan J. Robertson
Chief Judge

[Seal]

/s/ Paul H. Buchanan, Jr.
Presiding Judge

/s/ Robert H. Staton
Presiding Judge

/s/ Judge Robert B. Lybrook

/s/ Judge Joe W. Lowdermilk

/s/ Judge Patrick D. Sullivan

/s/ Judge Charles S. White

/s/ Judge George B. Hoffman, Jr.

/s/ Judge William I. Garrard

IN MEMORIAM

IN THE

COURT OF APPEALS OF INDIANA

RE: ADOPTION OF RESOLUTION OF THE COURT OF APPEALS OF INDIANA IN MEMORY OF THE LATE HONORABLE JOHN W. PFAFF

ORDER

The Court orders the foregoing Memorial Resolution spread of record upon the permanent records of this Court, and the Clerk of this Court is ordered to deliver a copy of said Memorial Resolution to the Reporter of this Court who is ordered to print and publish the same in the official Indiana Court of Appeals Reports.

IT IS FURTHER ORDERED that the Clerk of this Court transmit a copy of said Memorial Resolution under the seal of this Court, to the widow of the late Judge John W. Pfaff, Mrs. Odessa W. Pfaff, Rural Route 3, Box 209–480, Lakeview Drive, Eagle Lake, Edwardsburg, Michigan 49112.

IT IS FURTHER ORDERED that the Clerk of this Court transmit a copy of said Memorial Resolution to the Clerk of the Saint Joseph Circuit Court, South Bend, Indiana, 46601, who is instructed to spread said Memorial Resolution of Record.

Done at Indianapolis, Indiana, this fourteenth day of March, 1977.

/s/ Jonathan J. Robertson
Chief Judge

✝

XLVIII

Portrait courtesy of the Indiana Court of Appeals.

John Ambrose Kendall

~ 1907-1993 ~

- Born May 12, 1907, in Hendricks County, Indiana.

- Received a bachelor of law degree from Indiana University School of Law in 1931.

- Admitted to practice law before the Supreme Court of Indiana in 1931.

- Began practicing law in Hendricks County, Indiana.

- Elected prosecutor for the Fifty-fifth Circuit, serving from 1933 to 1939.

- Elected to the House of Representatives in the Indiana General Assembly from 1941 to 1944.

- Elected to represent Hendricks, Morgan and Owen counties as a state senator in the Indiana General Assembly from 1945 to 1952.

Continued ~

John Ambrose Kendall

 continued

- Received a doctorate of jurisprudence degree from Indiana University in 1951.

- Served on the Indiana Court of Appeals from 1953 to 1957.

- Appointed to the Indiana Toll Road Commission from 1957 to 1963.

- Served as president of the Indiana Bar Association from 1970 to 1971.

- Retired in 1987, after practicing law for fifty-six years.

- Died May 1, 1993, in Greencastle, Putnam County, Indiana.

In Memoriam

HONORABLE JOHN A. KENDALL

In Memoriam

HONORABLE JOHN A. KENDALL

The following Resolution was adopted as a memorial to the late John A. Kendall.

WHEREAS, the Honorable John A. Kendall, a resident of Greencastle, formerly of Danville, was a former Judge of the Appellate Court of Indiana; and

WHEREAS, it is with deep regret that we note the passing of Judge Kendall on May 1, 1993, whose active life spanned 85 years; and

WHEREAS, Judge Kendall was elected to the Appellate Court in November 1952; began his term on January 1, 1953; and served that Court until December 31, 1956; and

WHEREAS, he received his Bachelor of Laws degree from the Indiana University School of Law in 1931, was admitted to practice before the Supreme Court of Indiana the same year, and received his Doctorate of Jurisprudence from Indiana University in 1951; and

WHEREAS, Judge Kendall began the practice of law in Hendricks County, Indiana, was elected prosecutor and reelected twice to serve a total of six years; and subsequently was elected to two terms each in the Indiana House of Representatives and the Indiana Senate, where he rose to the Chairmanship of the Senate Budget Committee for five years; and

WHEREAS, he also served the people of Indiana in other positions by being twice appointed by Indiana Governors to the Indiana Toll Road Commission, including four years as its Chairman, and membership on the Indiana State Police Board; and

WHEREAS, Judge Kendall was a past president of the Indiana State Bar Association, and Hendricks County Republican Party Chairman, and a member of the Danville Friends Meeting, as well as a recipient of the Distinguished Alumnus Award from the Indiana University School of Law—Indianapolis, and twice proclaimed a Sagamore of the Wabash; and

WHEREAS, he served the State of Indiana with distinction during his four years as a Judge of the Appellate Court and during his 56 years in the practice of law; and

WHEREAS, Judge Kendall was married to Virginia Mattern Kendall and leaves her surviving as his widow; and also surviving him are a son, J. Richard Kendall; and a daughter, Ann Clark; and a brother, Kirk Kendall; and a sister, Sally Nicely; and

WHEREAS, his passing is a great loss to his community, our State, his family and friends.

IN MEMORIAM

NOW, THEREFORE BE IT RESOLVED, that Memorial Resolution be adopted by the Court of Appeals of Indiana and spread of record on the Order Book of this Court.

BE IT FURTHER RESOLVED, that the members of this court extend their sympathy to the widow, son, daughter, brother, sister, family and friends of this able lawyer and jurist; and that a copy of this Memorial Resolution be spread upon the record in the Order Book of the Hendricks County Circuit Court; and that a copy of the Memorial Resolution under seal of this court, be sent to his widow, Mrs. Virginia Mattern Kendall, 2210 West Seminary Street, Greencastle, Indiana, 46135.

Done at Indianapolis, Indiana, this 26th day of May, 1993.

(s) JOHN T. SHARPNACK
John T. Sharpnack
Chief Judge

(s) JOHN G. BAKER
John G. Baker
Presiding Judge

(s) V. SUE SHIELDS
V. Sue Shields
Presiding Judge

(s) GEORGE B. HOFFMAN, JR.
George B. Hoffman, Jr.
Presiding Judge

(s) STANLEY B. MILLER
Stanley B. Miller
Presiding Judge

(s) JONATHAN J. ROBERTSON
Judge Jonathan J. Robertson

(s) EDWARD W. NAJAM, JR.
Judge Edward W. Najam, Jr.

(s) PATRICK D. SULLIVAN
Judge Patrick D. Sullivan

(s) EZRA H. FRIEDLANDER
Judge Ezra H. Friedlander

(s) ROBERT H. STATON
Judge Robert H. Staton

(s) WILLIAM I. GARRARD
Judge William I. Garrard

(s) WILLIAM G. CONOVER
Judge William G. Conover

(s) LINDA L. CHEZEM
Judge Linda L. Chezem

(s) BETTY BARTEAU
Judge Betty Barteau

(s) ROBERT D. RUCKER
Judge Robert D. Rucker

HONORABLE JOHN A. KENDALL

ADOPTION OF RESOLUTION OF THE COURT OF APPEALS OF INDIANA IN MEMORY OF THE LATE

HONORABLE JOHN A. KENDALL

ORDER

The Court orders the foregoing Memorial Resolution spread of record upon the permanent records of this Court, and the Clerk of this Court is ordered to deliver a copy of said Memorial Resolution to the Reporter of this Court who is ordered to print and publish the same in the official Indiana Court of Appeals Reports.

IT IS FURTHER ORDERED that the Clerk of this Court transmit a copy of said Memorial Resolution, under seal of this Court, to the widow of the late Judge John A. Kendall, Mrs. Virginia Mattern Kendall, 210 West Seminary Street, Greencastle, Indiana, 46135.

IT IS FURTHER ORDERED that the Clerk of this Court transmit a copy of said Memorial Resolution to the Clerk of the Hendricks Circuit Court, Danville, Indiana 46122, who is instructed to spread said Memorial Resolution of Record.

Done at Indianapolis, Indiana, this 26th day of May, 1993.

(s) JOHN T. SHARPNACK
John T. Sharpnack
Chief Judge

Portrait courtesy of the Indiana Court of Appeals.

Stanley B. Miller

1929-1994

- Born April 23, 1929, in Indianapolis, Marion County, Indiana.

- Received a bachelor's degree from Butler University (Indianapolis, Indiana) in 1949.

- Received a law degree from Indiana University School of Law at Indianapolis in 1953.

- Admitted to practice law before the Indiana Supreme Court in 1953.

- Served in the United States Army Counter Intelligence Corps during the Korean War.

- Served as a Deputy Attorney General for Indiana from 1955 to 1965.

Continued

Stanley B. Miller

~ continued ~

- Served as chief counsel for the Marion County prosecuting attorney from 1968 to 1969.

- Appointed United States attorney for the Southern District of Indiana in December of 1969 and served until 1975.

- Taught religious school at Congregation Beth-El Zedeck for seventeen years.

- Appointed to the Indiana Court of Appeals on August 1, 1978, and served until his death.

- Died June 20, 1994, in Indianapolis, Marion County, Indiana.

Court of Appeals of Indiana

In Memoriam

HONORABLE STANLEY B. MILLER

In Memoriam

HONORABLE STANLEY B. MILLER

The following Resolution was adopted as a memorial to the late Stanley B. Miller.

WHEREAS, the Honorable Stanley B. Miller, a resident of Indianapolis, was a Judge of the Court of Appeals of Indiana; and

WHEREAS, it is with deep regret that we note the passing of Judge Miller at age 65 on June 20, 1994; and

WHEREAS, Judge Miller was appointed to the Court of Appeals of Indiana on August 1, 1978, retained by the electorate in November, 1980 and 1990, and served until his death; and

WHEREAS, Judge Miller received his undergraduate degree from Butler University and his law degree from Indiana University School of Law at Indianapolis in 1953 and was admitted to practice before the Supreme Court of Indiana the same year; and

WHEREAS, Judge Miller served in the U.S. Army Counter Intelligence Corps; served the people of Indiana from 1955 to 1965 as a Deputy Attorney General, in the private practice of law, and as a deputy prosecutor and later as Chief Counsel for the Marion County Prosecutor's office; and was appointed U.S. Attorney for the Southern District of Indiana in December of 1969 and reentered the private practice of law in 1975; and

WHEREAS, Judge Miller was member of the American Legion Veterans of Foreign Wars, a past master of Monument Masonic Lodge # 657, Scottish Rite and Murat Shrine, a former board member of the Bureau of Jewish Education, having taught religious school for 17 years at Congregation Beth–El Zedeck, the Indiana State Bar Association, and the Indiana Judges Association; and

WHEREAS, Judge Miller was married to Mary Zendell and leaves her surviving as his widow; and also is survived by four sons, Gary Miller, Mark Miller, Leo Miller, Mathew Miller, and two grandchildren; and

WHEREAS, his passing is a great loss to his community, our State, his family, friends, and this Court.

NOW, THEREFORE, BE IT RESOLVED, that this Memorial Resolution be adopted by the Court of Appeals of Indiana and spread of record on the Order Book of this Court.

BE IT FURTHER RESOLVED, that the members of this Court extend their sympathy to the widow, sons, family and friends of this able lawyer and jurist; and that a copy of this Memorial Resolution be spread upon the record in the Order Book of the Marion County Circuit Court; and that a copy of the Memorial Resolu-

IN MEMORIAM

tion, under seal of this Court, be sent to his widow, Mrs. Mary Z. Miller, 8656 Cricket Tree Lane, Indianapolis, Indiana 46260.

Done at Indianapolis, Indiana, this 28th day of February, 1995

JOHN T. SHARPNACK

John T. Sharpnack
Chief Judge and
Presiding Judge, Fifth District

JOHN G. BAKER

John G. Baker
Presiding Judge, First District

PATRICK D. SULLIVAN

Patrick D. Sullivan
Presiding Judge, Second District

ROBERT H. STATON

Robert H. Staton
Presiding Judge, Third District

LINDA L. CHEZEM

Linda L. Chezem
Presiding Judge, Fourth District

JONATHAN J. ROBERTSON

Judge Jonathan J. Robertson

EDWARD W. NAJAM

Judge Edward W. Najam

EZRA H. FRIEDLANDER

Judge Ezra H. Friedlander

JAMES S. KIRSCH

Judge James S. Kirsch

GEORGE B. HOFFMAN

Judge George B. Hoffman

WILLIAM I. GARRARD

Judge William I. Garrard

PATRICIA A. RILEY

Judge Patricia A. Riley

CARR L. DARDEN

Judge Carr L. Darden

BETTY BARTEAU

Judge Betty Barteau

ROBERT D. RUCKER

Judge Robert D. Rucker

Portrait courtesy of the Indiana Court of Appeals.

James Boner Young

~ 1928-1998 ~

- Born May 5, 1928, in Kankakee, Illinois.

- Received a bachelor's degree from Franklin College (Franklin, Indiana) in 1950.

- Served in the United States Army Counter Intelligence Corps during the Korean War from 1951 to 1953.

- Earned a law degree from Indiana University School of Law— Bloomington in 1955.

- Admitted to the Indiana bar in 1955.

- Served as the City Attorney for Franklin, Wayne County, Indiana from 1958 to 1962.

Continued

James Boner Young

 continued

- Served as the County Attorney for Johnson County, Indiana, from 1966 to 1975.

- Elected State Senator in 1966, serving until 1970.

- Served as Special Assistant to the Governor for Legislative Affairs from 1973 to 1975.

- Appointed United States Attorney for the Southern District of Indiana in 1975.

- Reentered the private practice of law in 1977.

- Appointed to the Indiana Court of Appeals on August 1, 1978, serving until 1988.

- Died August 29, 1998, in Florida.

In Memoriam

HONORABLE JAMES B. YOUNG

The following Resolution was adopted as a memorial to the late James B. Young.

WHEREAS, the Honorable James B. Young, a resident of Naples, Florida, was a Judge of the Court of Appeals of Indiana; and

WHEREAS, it is with deep regret that we note the passing of Judge Young at age 70 on August 29, 1998; and

WHEREAS, Judge Young was appointed to the Court of Appeals of Indiana on August 1, 1978, retained by the electorate in November, 1980, and served until his retirement in 1988; and

WHEREAS, Judge Young received his undergraduate degree from Franklin College and his law degree from Indiana University School of Law—Bloomington in 1955 and was admitted to practice before the Supreme Court of Indiana the same year; and

WHEREAS, Judge Young served in the U.S. Army Counter Intelligence Corps from 1951 to 1953; served the people of Indiana as the City Attorney for the City of Franklin, Indiana from 1958 to 1962, as County Attorney for Johnson County from 1966 to 1975, as State Senator from 1966 to 1970, as Special Assistant to the Governor for Legislative Affairs from 1973 to 1975, and in the private practice of law from 1955 to 1975; was appointed the U.S. Attorney for the Southern District of Indiana in 1975 and reentered the private practice of law in 1977; and

WHEREAS, Judge Young was a Korean War Veteran, a life member of the Benevolent and Protective Order of Elks, a member of the American Judicature Society and Association of Former United States Attorneys, a member of the Indianapolis, Johnson County (President in 1967), 7th Circuit, Florida, and Indiana State Bar Associations, and was named a Sagamore of the Wabash by Governor Otis Bowen; and

WHEREAS, Judge Young is survived by Pamela Auxter Young, three daughters, Melinda Finlinson, Sarah Henry, Carrie Bryson, a son, Dr. Matthew Young, five grandchildren, and two step-grandchildren; and

WHEREAS, his passing is a loss to his community, our State, his family, friends and this Court.

NOW, THEREFORE, BE IT RESOLVED, that this Memorial Resolution be adopted by the Court of Appeals of Indiana and spread on record on the Order Book of this Court.

BE IT FURTHER RESOLVED, that the members of this Court extend their sympathy to Pamela A. Young and to the daughters, son, family and friends of this able lawyer and jurist and that a copy of the Memorial Resolution, under seal of this Court, be sent to Pamela A. Young and to his daughters and son.

XLIX

IN MEMORIAM

Done at Indianapolis, Indiana, this 7th day of November, 1998.

John T. Sharpnack, Chief Judge and Presiding Judge, Fifth District
Edward W. Najam, Jr., Presiding Judge, First District
Patrick D. Sullivan, Presiding Judge, Second District
William I. Garrard, Presiding Judge, Third District
Carr L. Darden, Presiding Judge, Fourth District

Judge John G. Baker
Judge L. Mark Bailey
Judge Ezra H. Friedlander
Judge James S. Kirsch
Judge Sanford M. Brook
Judge Robert H. Staton
Judge Patricia A. Riley
Judge Melissa S. Mattingly
Judge Robert D. Rucker
Judge Margret G. Robb

†

Portrait courtesy of the Indiana Court of Appeals.

Joseph Owen Carson, II

1909-1998

- Born April 14, 1909, in Indianapolis, Marion County, Indiana.

- Received a bachelor's degree from Indiana University in 1930.

- Earned a law degree from Indiana University School of Law—Bloomington in 1932.

- Admitted to the Indiana bar in 1932.

- Worked in private law practice in Indianapolis from 1932 to 1942.

- Served in the United States Army Air Corps during World War II in special services and with the Judge Advocate's Division from 1942 until 1946.

- Remained in the Air Force Reserves and retired with the rank of lieutenant colonel.

Continued

Joseph Owen Carson, II

 continued

- Returned to private law practice in North Vernon, Jennings County, Indiana, from 1947 to 1963.

- Served as city attorney of North Vernon in 1948.

- Served as county attorney of Jennings County from 1949 to 1950.

- Elected prosecuting attorney for the Sixth Judicial District in Indiana, in 1950.

- Elected to the Indiana Court of Appeals in November 1962 and served from January 1, 1963, to December 31, 1970.

- Served as the Jennings County Circuit Court judge from 1973 to 1978.

- Died November 14, 1998, in North Vernon, Jennings County, Indiana.

In Memoriam

HONORABLE JOSEPH O. CARSON II

The following Resolution was adopted as a memorial to the late Joseph O. Carson II.

WHEREAS, the Honorable Joseph O. Carson II, a resident of North Vernon, was a Judge of the Court of Appeals of Indiana; and

WHEREAS, it is with deep regret that we note the passing of Judge Carson at age 89 on November 14, 1998; and

WHEREAS, Judge Carson was elected to the Court of Appeals of Indiana in November 1962 and served from January 1, 1963 to December 31, 1970; and

WHEREAS, Judge Carson received his undergraduate degree from Indiana University and his law degree from Indiana University School of Law–Bloomington in 1932 and was admitted to practice before the Supreme Court of Indiana the same year; and

WHEREAS, Judge Carson served in the U.S. Army Air Corps during World War II in special services and with the Judge Advocate's Division; remained in the reserves after the war and retired as a lieutenant colonel; served the people of Indiana in the private practice of law in Indianapolis from 1932 to 1942 and in North Vernon from 1947 to 1963; as the Jennings County Circuit Court Judge from 1973 to 1978; as the North Vernon City Court Judge; as the prosecutor for Scott and Jennings Counties; and again in the private practice of law in North Vernon from 1979 until he retired; and

WHEREAS, Judge Carson was a World War II Veteran, a member of the North Vernon Presbyterian Church, the North Vernon Masonic Lodge No. 59, the Scottish Rite of Indianapolis, the Gamma Eta Gamma legal fraternity, a past president and secretary of the Jennings–Scott County Bar Association, a member of the Indiana and American Bar Associations and the Indiana Judges Association; and

WHEREAS, Judge Carson was married to Elisabeth Chastain and leaves her surviving as his widow; and also is survived by two daughters, Sarah E. Gierzynski and Olga Pelance, four grandchildren, and four great-grandchildren; and

WHEREAS, his passing is a loss to his community, our State, his family, friends and this Court.

NOW, THEREFORE, BE IT RESOLVED, that this Memorial Resolution be adopted by the Court of Appeals of Indiana and spread of record on the Order Book of this Court.

BE IT FURTHER RESOLVED, that the members of this Court extend their sympathy to the widow, daughters, family and friends of this able lawyer and jurist and that a copy of the Memorial Resolution, under seal of the Court, be sent to his widow, Mrs. Elisabeth C. Carson, 526 South Jennings Street, North Vernon, Indiana 47265.

IN MEMORIAM

Done at Indianapolis, Indiana, this 8th day of December, 1998.

John T. Sharpnack, Chief Judge and Presiding Judge, Fifth District
Edward W. Najam, Jr., Presiding Judge, First District
Patrick D. Sullivan, Presiding Judge, Second District
William I. Garrard, Presiding Judge, Third District
Carr L. Darden, Presiding Judge, Fourth District

Judge John G. Baker
Judge L. Mark Bailey
Judge Ezra H. Friedlander
Judge James S. Kirsch
Judge Sanford M. Brook
Judge Robert H. Staton
Judge Patricia A. Riley
Judge Melissa S. Mattingly
Judge Robert D. Rucker
Judge Margret G. Robb

†

Portrait courtesy of the Indiana Court of Appeals.

Robert W. Neal

1924-2000

- Born May 14, 1924, in Clay City, Clay County, Indiana.

- Graduated from Clay City High School in 1941.

- Served as an infantryman in the United States Army from 1942 to 1945, fighting in the Battle of the Bulge and receiving the Purple Heart.

- Received his law degree from Indiana University School of Law—Bloomington in 1951.

- Worked in private practice of law in Brazil, Clay County, Indiana, from 1951 to 1970.

- Served as the Clay County Circuit Court judge from 1970 to 1979.

- Appointed to the Indiana Court of Appeals by Governor Otis R. Bowen on October 1, 1979, serving until his retirement in 1989.

- Died November 12, 2000, in Brazil, Clay County, Indiana.

Indiana Court of Appeals

In Memoriam
HONORABLE
ROBERT W. NEAL

Indianapolis, Indiana
January 8, 2001

In Memoriam

HONORABLE ROBERT W. NEAL

The following Resolution was adopted as a memorial to the late Robert W. Neal.

WHEREAS, the Honorable Robert W. Neal, a resident of Brazil, Indiana, was a Judge of the Court of Appeals of Indiana; and

WHEREAS, it is with deep regret that we note the passing of Judge Neal at age 76 on November 12, 2000; and

WHEREAS, Judge Neal was appointed to the Court of Appeals of Indiana on October 1, 1979 and served until his retirement in 1989; and

WHEREAS, Judge Neal received his law degree from Indiana University School of Law–Bloomington in 1951 and was admitted to practice before the Supreme Court of Indiana the same year; and

WHEREAS, Judge Neal served in the U.S. Army during World War II as an infantryman; fought in the Battle of the Bulge, receiving the Purple Heart; served the people of Indiana in the private practice of law in Brazil from 1951 to 1970; and as the Clay County Circuit Court Judge from 1970 to 1979; and

WHEREAS, Judge Neal was a World War II Veteran, a member of the Brazil First United Methodist Church, the American Legion, the Brazil Lodge of the Benevolent and Protective Order of Elks, the Exchange Club, the Thursday Men's Club, the Clay County School Board, the Indiana State Bar Association, and the Indiana Judges Association, and a recipient of the Sagamore of the Wabash; and

WHEREAS, Judge Neal was married to Margaret A. Singer and leaves her surviving as his widow; and also is survived by two daughters, Jennifer Neal and Ellen Packard, and one son, Robert Neal, and three grandchildren; and

WHEREAS, his passing is a loss to his community, our State, his family, friends, and this Court.

NOW, THEREFORE, BE IT RESOLVED, that this Memorial Resolution be adopted by the Court of Appeals of Indiana and spread of record on the Order Book of this Court.

BE IT FURTHER RESOLVED, that the members of this Court extend their sympathy to the widow, to the daughters, son, family and friends of this able lawyer and jurist and that a copy of the Memorial Resolution, under seal of this Court, be sent to his widow.

IN MEMORIAM

Done at Indianapolis, Indiana, this 8th day of January, 2001.

John T. Sharpnack
Chief Judge and Presiding Judge,
Fifth District

John G. Baker
Presiding Judge, First District

James S. Kirsch
Presiding Judge, Second District

Sanford M. Brook
Presiding Judge, Third District

Melissa S. Mattingly
Presiding Judge, Fourth District

Judge L. Mark Bailey

Judge Michael P. Barnes

Judge Carr L. Darden

Judge Ezra H. Friedlander

Judge Paul D. Mathias

Judge Edward W. Najam, Jr.

Judge Patricia A. Riley

Judge Margret G. Robb

Judge Patrick D. Sullivan

Judge Nancy H. Vaidik

†

Index

Index